DATE DUE

Demco, Inc. 38-293

Finding the STORY

Behind the NUMBERS

Were there to be a parade of all educators, which by count, I'm sure would circle the globe, the leader of that parade would be my wife, Keni. In my 45 years as part of the greatest profession on the face of the earth, I have never witnessed more passion for the work of educating children than she has. Equaled by many, I'm sure, but never surpassed, she truly gives "quality" a new definition. Raising the bar is her norm. Failure is not an option. This book is dedicated to Keni and her work.

Finding the Story Behind the Numbers

A Tool-Based Guide for Evaluating Educational Programs

James Cox

CORWIN PRESS
A SAGE Publications Company
Thousand Oaks, CA 91320

For information:

Corwin Press
A Sage Publications Company
2455 Teller Road
Thousand Oaks, California 91320
www.corwinpress.com

Sage Publications Ltd.
1 Oliver's Yard
55 City Road
London EC1Y 1SP
United Kingdom

Sage Publications India Pvt. Ltd.
B-42, Panchsheel Enclave
Post Box 4109
New Delhi 110 017 India

Printed in the United States of America

Library of Congress Cataloging-in-Publication Data

Cox, James, 1938-
Finding the story behind the numbers: A tool-based guide for evaluating educational programs/James Cox.
    p. cm.
Includes bibliographical references and index.
ISBN 1-4129-4243-8 or 978-1-4129-4243-0 (cloth)
ISBN 1-4129-4244-6 or 978-1-4129-4244-7 (pbk.)
  1. Educational evaluation-United States. I. Title.
LB2822.75.C69 2007
379.1'58—dc22   2006020220

This book is printed on acid-free paper.

06 07 08 09 10 10 9 8 7 6 5 4 3 2 1

Acquisitions Editor:	Rachel Livsey
Editorial Assistant:	Phyllis Cappello
Copy Editor:	Teresa Herlinger
Typesetter:	C&M Digitals (P) Ltd.
Proofreader:	Dennis Webb
Indexer:	Rick Hurd
Cover Designer:	Monique Hahn
Graphic Designer:	Lisa Miller

Contents

Preface

Primarily written for educational leaders and leadership teams, this book is intended to provide a different approach to dealing with high-stakes accountability and school improvement from what has been normally taken. Program improvement is hard work! School reform cannot be legislated from an external source. It occurs from the inside out, not from the outside in. It requires knowledge and skills, more than a small amount of commitment, acceptance of responsibility for the quality of our work, and extraordinary patience . . . all occurring in the face of a thunderous crowd of naysayers, convinced we are not up to the task.

The manner in which we frame the work of improving our schools is critical to our success. Observe successful athletic coaches at work. There is offense; there is defense; there are the specific skills within each; there are each player's strengths and weaknesses; there are the rules of the game; and there is the art of bringing several individuals together to create a team. There is a purpose for every action that a successful coach takes, and *that action fits within the framework that the coach has defined for himself or herself.* Why the italics for emphasis? Because without a good framework or structure, action becomes aimless, little more than a random search for solutions.

In our profession, structures and frameworks abound. We organize schools by grade levels—or not, depending on the structure we adopt; we write curriculum guides, align schedules to fulfill mandates, and develop lesson plans, whether five-step, seven-step, or some other. The point is, we have a multitude of structures and frameworks that we use to routinize our work, focus our efforts, and ensure compliance.

Just as a coach needs a framework within which to work and teachers need frameworks when working with students, so do we educators need a framework for successfully improving our schools. Every action we take should fit into a well-designed outline that explains why we're doing what we're doing, every step along the way. Bottom line: We need a framework for producing quality!

As we establish this framework, we must remind ourselves that successful school improvement is not based on any one criterion. It does not happen because we have curriculum standards. It cannot be found solely in our new instructional materials. It does not occur just because we have an enlightened leader or a group of well-trained teachers. And most of all, we don't get school improvement because someone on high deems it so. Where then, does the path to school improvement reside? Answer: School improvement resides within a sound framework—a framework focused on the quality of our work.

This book offers a three-pronged framework for doing the work of school improvement. I title it, "The Three Faces of Quality." Our job is to improve continuously each of these faces: (1) teacher effectiveness, (2) program elements, and (3) leadership. The book posits that *effective teachers + effective program elements + effective leadership = a high-quality instructional program.* The "three faces" define program quality. Improving the three faces improves program quality. Improving program quality improves student achievement. It's that clear!

Chapter 1 addresses four important concepts that are necessary precursors to presenting "The Three Faces of Quality." Chapter 2 discusses each of the three faces in detail, providing tools to assist a leadership team to work within that "face." Chapter 3 extends our discussion from the three faces to two important stages of any newly developed program, (1) planning and (2) capacity building. Tools are provided here as well. Chapter 4 challenges a school or district leadership team to move forward by providing a step-by-step process. All tools introduced in the earlier chapters are provided for photocopying in Resource A, at the end of the book.

ACKNOWLEDGMENTS

This book is not the result of an event; it is the result of a process—a long process. It took 45 years to get here. There are specific people during my many professional years who played such an important role. I'm pleased to have a chance to reflect on those to whom I am grateful. And of course, there are many more. I want to acknowledge them here, because developing the content of this book began in 1960 and continues to this day. Without the 45 years of experience, there would be no book. I offer my thanks to the following people:

Paul Baker, my first principal in Aurora, Colorado, early 1960s, who "taught" me to love teaching.

Dr. Sam Gates, Dean of the Graduate School at Colorado State College (now Northern Colorado University), who invited me in 1966 to become part of a new doctoral program in educational research.

Dr. Pat Carrigan, Director of Research in the Ann Arbor, Michigan, public school system, who hired and guided me through my first experience as a research consultant in 1968.

Dr. Joe Dionne, Vice President and General Manager of CTB/McGraw-Hill, who had the "novel" idea in 1970 that the company should offer evaluation services (since few knew anything about evaluation at that time). I was invited to become a part of that venture.

Dr. Gordon Footman, Los Angeles County Office of Education, who taught me well the art of consulting, and Dr. John Martois, same organization, who taught me well the art of statistics.

Cynthia Grennan, Superintendent of the Anaheim Union High School District, and Bruce Hauger, Assistant Superintendent, who were among the first to risk hiring a Director of Research and Evaluation in 1982, a position not often found in middle-sized school districts at that time. I learned the practical aspects of my craft while in this position.

Dr. Tom Harvey, leader of the School of Organizational Management at the University of La Verne, California, and the incredible faculty (Don, Barbara, Pat, Bill, Manny, Carol, Larry, Don, et al.) who supported my learning the ins and outs of being an educational leader, a time when I learned there was something more to leading than understanding test scores.

To the staffs at Francis Polytechnic High School, Los Angeles Unified School District, and those in the Curriculum and Instruction Division in the Monterey County Office of Education, California: Thank you for "extending" my career and giving me the gift of allowing me to hone my craft, when by all counts, I should have been in a rocking chair. So to Jan Fries-Martinez, principal at Poly, and to Kari Yeater, Adrian Meckel, Nancy Kotowski, and Bill Barr of the Monterey County Office of Education, a hearty "thank you for allowing my flame to burn a bit longer."

And finally, I thank all the teachers and administrators who have allowed me to be a small part of their professional lives for a day or two, sometimes much longer, to share some ideas, to respond to their inquiries, and to accept their challenges that on occasion (more times than I want to admit), I was wrong! To you thousands, it was you who were an important catalyst for the book's content.

Corwin Press gratefully acknowledges the contributions of the following reviewers:

Victoria Bernhardt
Executive Director
Education for the Future
Chico, CA

Danny Hal Strain
Principal
Clarke N. Johnsen Junior High
Tooele, UT

Marie Blum
Superintendent
Canaseraga Central School District
Canaseraga, NY

Terry Quam
K–8 Principal
Menno Elementary School
Menno, SD

Bruce Deterding
Principal
Wichita High School South
Wichita, KS

AUTHOR'S NOTE: DILEMMA OF A CONSULTANT

I am an educational consultant, full time for about nine years and part time for many more while either a university faculty member or a school district director of research and evaluation. I now have one foot in and one foot out of retirement, more in than out. My areas of "expertise" have been educational evaluation, testing, accountability, and assisting schools and districts to become "data-driven organizations." Most folks in the small circle in which I have done my work would say that I'm pretty good at what I do, or did. Accolades aside, however, I have to ask myself, "What kind of impact have I really made?"

In reflecting on this question just three or four years ago, I had to respond, "Not much!" As good as I was at what I was doing, I could find little evidence of my influence on the effectiveness of educators as they struggled to deal with the saturation of state and federal accountability mandates, challenges, rewards, sanctions, threats, or whatever you want to call them. So, I pursued an answer to the more important issue, "Why not?"

I revisited my work from the early days of norm-referenced testing to the more current No Child Left Behind requirements. I reread the many position papers I had written. I carefully studied my seminar content, designed and redesigned over the past 10 to 15 years. I read the never-published book I had written on how to work successfully with high-stakes test data . . . still no answers as to what the mystery piece might be.

Then one day, no different from any other, I was speaking to a group, doing the exercises of which I was so proud and that everyone seemed to enjoy, when it hit. You might say I had an epiphany. I knew I had it. I believe I now know why all the student test data in the world are not making more than a small dent in the practices of most educational institutions.

The purpose of this writing is to try to convince you that the "something" missing is absolutely essential if we are to be successful in the elusive educational reform movement. Yes, it has to do with data and the collecting of data, but I believe you're in for a bit of a surprise. I hope you choose to come along. I believe it will be a good ride.

About the Author

James Cox taught mathematics, coached, and was a site administrator before receiving his doctorate from Northern Colorado University in 1968. He worked for CTB/McGraw-Hill, the publishing company's testing arm, during the first half of the 1970s, returning to public education as an evaluation consultant for the Los Angeles County Office of Education in 1975. During the 1980s, he was Director of Research and Evaluation for the Anaheim Union High School District. He was on the executive staff of the California School Leadership Academy and coauthored two staff development modules on testing and accountability. Until the mid-1990s, he was Associate Professor at the University of La Verne (ULV) in southern California, working exclusively in ULV's doctoral program in educational leadership.

In 1996, he and his wife, Dr. Keni Cox, started a consultant firm, JK Educational Associates, and this work has continued to the present. In that same year, he published his first Corwin Press book, *Your Opinion, Please!*, which is a guide for educators who are faced with designing questionnaires.

James's area of experience and expertise is educational testing, program evaluation, and the management of educational change. Over the years, he has developed seminars for virtually every stakeholder group in the field of education: teacher leaders, site administrators, superintendents, and school boards. When practitioners are asked about James's skills in this area, their most frequent response is, "He makes the complex easy to understand."

Currently, his work focuses on assisting educators in dealing with various aspects of educational accountability, NCLB style. James lives the credo of "continuous improvement" and makes no apologies for having "failed" at retirement.

The Four Pillars of Program Quality

Considering the title of this book, *Finding the Story Behind the Numbers: A Tool-Based Guide for Evaluating Educational Programs,* it may seem a bit strange that you won't get to the meat of the topic immediately. Undoubtedly, this will be the longest introduction of any book you've ever read. But there is a very good reason for this approach.

The accountability movement, with its resultant data barrage, has hit a sensitive spot for many educators. Few of us were ever formally taught what to do when our school's high-stakes test scores crossed our desks. We may have had a statistics course or two, but real-world usage eluded us when we were university students. We have attended on-the-job staff development sessions focusing on test usage, but often left frustrated either by impractical content (*"When on earth are we supposed to find the time to do all this?"*) or feeling overwhelmed after being handed a notebook full of numbers. The bottom line is that many of us really lack a framework to work with data effectively.

When we embrace an effective framework, we can answer questions like . . .

"When the test results arrive, what steps do I take to work with them if I am to make a difference in my school?"

"What do these scores tell me about the quality of instruction at my school?"

"What are the reasons for our school's scores being as low (or as high) as they are?"

"Is there a difference between data that are important and data that are useful? Are data that we consider important, by their very nature, automatically useful?"

(Continued)

(Continued)

This introductory chapter presents a response to questions like those above and suggests a framework and rationale for tackling head on the pressure-filled test score arena. The presentation takes the form of four concepts that necessarily precede doing the work of this book. The four concepts provide a cornerstone for understanding why the book takes the approach that it does. When the reader internalizes the content of this chapter, then the title of the book takes on a whole new meaning. One of the first "aha's" is to see the need to define what we mean by "a high-quality educational program." If you're going along for this ride, understanding these four concepts is a must.

1. Working with test results effectively requires moving through a four-step process.

2. Test scores result the way they do for six reasons. The quality of our programs is only one of the six.

3. There are data that are important and data that are useful. They are typically not the same data. We must be able to distinguish importance from utility.

4. There is a direct relationship between the quality of our work and the quality of student achievement.

CONCEPT 1: USING TEST RESULTS—A FOUR-STEP PROCESS

Working with test scores effectively requires that educators establish a process for doing so. This process must allow us to progress through a prescribed set of steps, focusing on the quality of our programs rather than continuously attending to the political pressure of raising test scores. It will be shown shortly that these two ideas, focusing on *quality* and attending to *test scores,* are not the same thing. I'd like to present for your consideration the four steps that I deem essential. They are no panacea, but they do keep us focused, while at the same time keeping the scores in perspective.

Step 1: Establishing the Environment

Step 1 is less a step than a starting point, but it is so important that I have labeled it as Step 1. As leaders we must establish an environment in which our staff *knows and believes* that working with high-stakes test scores is very important work. Taking a proactive approach rather than reacting to external forces is the goal of Step 1. When we're told that something is important, but deep down we don't really believe it, we're going to end up giving it a puny effort.

I know of no educator who is thrilled at the notion of being judged solely by the results of a test. We do so much complaining that we often fail to acknowledge, "that's the way it is." Reacting in such a way often results in our stakeholders' viewing us as crybabies, afraid to be held accountable for doing good work with their kids. When our stakeholders view us this way, all we're doing is widening the credibility gap between us and those whom we serve. Accountability is here to stay and regardless of how unfair we believe some of these practices to be, we've got to ready ourselves for the challenge.

The attitudes we carry with us will go far in determining the manner in which we do this work. The principal cannot give a half-hearted effort in encouraging his or her staff to take this work seriously and expect success. Creating a positive environment when working with test results does not happen by osmosis or because the boss deems it so. A healthy environment must be planned and initiated, with no excuses or "cop-outs." A healthy environment acknowledges that improvement is not only possible—it is a professional obligation.

Step 2: Working With the Data

Step 2 is the point at which the numbers—the data from testing—are at center stage. The number-crunching step progresses from summarizing the data to establishing student needs. Though not the focus of this book, to retain continuity and enrich our understanding, a brief description is supplied here.

Summarizing the Data

Summarizing the data means nothing more than putting the data in a user-friendly format. Holcomb (2004) supports this notion when she asserts, "How the data looks does matter" (p. 91). Folks who don't work with data for a living and are exposed on occasion to information, such as test scores, need to feel comfortable with the numbers; comfort comes from less, not more, data. But, of course, the "less" must be the most important of the data available. Test scores often come to the educator in the form of computer printouts of various types with the accompanying admonition to "do something with it." Or they may arrive bound inside a pretty cover, full of graphs and tables suitable for display, but extremely difficult to use as a tool for analysis. Normally, there are too many numbers, too many graphs, and too many pages. Thus, "do something with it" is often met with "???????"

Because there are so much data resulting from a typical testing program (multiple content areas; multiple grades, multiple years; multiple groups and subgroups; etc.), we must first consider what are the most important data to know and then to deal with that information (Johnson, 2002). When we screen out that which is less important to us, we can eventually hold the important stuff in the palm of our hand. These are the data that promote understanding. Think of data summary as creating a funnel, wide at the top and very small at the bottom. Loads of data are poured into the top, but only the most important pieces come through at the bottom.

Figure 1.1 Data Funnel

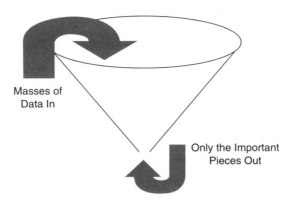

Masses of
Data In

Only the Important
Pieces Out

Analyzing the Data

The second process in Step 2 of the four steps is analysis. Analyzing the data simply asks us to answer the question, "What do these data tell us about the achievement levels of our students?" Though we often think otherwise, this is not a complex step. When we hear the word "analysis," we tend to think we need five courses in statistics to do the work. Such is not the case. Data analysis is a very common-sense issue. For example, we look at the data and conclude that we're doing better in primary reading than in intermediate reading, but we're performing better in intermediate math than in primary math; our girls are performing consistently higher than our boys; and students who have been with us at least two years are performing 10 to 12 percentile ranks higher than those who have not been with us as long. That's all there is to it. Analyzing the data prepares us to move to the next point: establishing a priority of student need.

Determining Needs

Once we understand what the data say, we draw a conclusion that states, "These are our students' needs." This brings closure to Step 2. We have determined content needs, needs by grade, and/or subgroup needs. We make statements such as, "We have a need in reading in our primary grades; we have a need in math in Grades 4, 5, and 6; we have a need in reading with our boys; we have a need in Grade 6 across the board."

Determining need does not result in problem solving or devising solutions. Closure for Step 2 does not suggest a need for more materials or for additional staff development. That comes later. Establishing need focuses only on the learning needs of students.

Step 3: Establishing Cause

Identifying the causes of the test scores is by far the most important step in the four-step process. *It is also the step that is most often neglected.* At this point we answer questions such as, "Why do we have a need in reading in our primary grades? In math at the intermediate level? In reading with our boys? In Grade 6?"

Using our best professional judgment, we identify those causes *that are within our contro*l; the premise is that by addressing these causes, via an appropriate action plan, improved student achievement will result.

Here's the bottom line: Step 3, Establishing Cause, is the most important of the four steps because when a staff accurately identifies the causes of need, an appropriate plan for improving quality will naturally follow. When a staff *in*accurately identifies the causes, the improvement plan can easily move the school in the wrong direction.

Concept 2 below is entitled "Why Test Scores Result the Way They Do," and provides a template for establishing cause. This section clusters the causes of test scores into two groups: pollutants and program quality. Pollutants are those variables that affect test scores but have nothing to do with the quality of the instructional program. Program quality is the focus of this book—defining it, describing it, measuring it, and drawing conclusions about its current state. An understanding of Concept 2 is essential for successfully completing Step 3 of The Four-Step Process.

Step 4: Developing the Improvement Plan

The most important thing to remember about Step 4 is this: Write a plan to address cause. Never write a plan to improve test scores. The plan should result in our doing something better, not necessarily in doing something different.

If continuously improving the overall quality of our programs is our goal, we must refrain from focusing on the results, and keep our eye on what we believe *caused* the results. If the causal factors we identified in Step 3 are accurate (at least partially), we will be headed toward improvement. If the factors we identify are not the right ones, our plan will probably go up in smoke.

From the long list of possible causes identified in Step 3 (see Concept 2 below for how this list is created), identify the ones that you believe are the most important, realizing that you can't deal with all of them. Your improvement plan will focus on eliminating or drastically reducing each of these causal factors.

CONCEPT 2: WHY TEST SCORES RESULT THE WAY THEY DO

Step 3 of the four-step process introduced the importance of establishing cause—that is, "Why did our results turn out the way they did?" Establishing cause is the focus of Concept 2.

One of the most common uses for test scores is to evaluate the quality of educational programs or to compare scores from one testing point to another to assess "growth." If the scores do not support the progress we are hoping to see, a common conclusion is that some limitations exist within the instructional program and that "fixing" is in order. That is in fact an inappropriate conclusion. Test scores only tell us "what is." All they give is a status report. Our response to the test results must be to answer the question, "Why?" Discovering the "why" requires further investigation. We must never assume cause from a score.

When educators or community members decide to "fix" a program based on test scores alone, they are assuming that the only variable that affects test scores is program quality. This is not the case. Scores result the way they do for six reasons: student demographics; physical environment in which the tests are taken; attitudes of the teachers and students toward the testing program; students' test-taking skills; alignment of curriculum content with test content; and program quality. Thus, when test scores for a school are reported, we should immediately know that to infer something about the quality of the program is inappropriate.

Below is a brief discussion of these six reasons, continuously reminding us that test scores by themselves do not point to cause.

Six Reasons

Demographics

Demographic variables include English proficiency, mobility of the school population, and socioeconomic status or degree of affluence of the students.

English proficiency. The impact of English proficiency is obvious. When a student has limited English skills and takes a test in English, the resulting score will not measure what the student knows in the area being tested. For example, I do not know a language other than English, but I can read very well. If I were to take a reading test in any other language than English, I would score close to the chance level. Those who would then conclude that I lack reading skills or that the educational program being employed to teach me reading is weak are simply not using common sense.

Mobility. When a school population is highly mobile, there are many students whose test scores are not a result of the educational program of the school in which the students now reside. To combine these scores (be they high or low) with those from the more stable population diminishes the accuracy of any conclusion drawn about the quality of the instructional program at that school. Remember, scores can change from one year to the next because the student population changes.

Socioeconomics. There is a predictable link between the socioeconomics of students and their resulting test scores. While this phenomenon is *never to be interpreted as a cause-and-effect relationship*, the connection is there, nevertheless. For example, in the current California testing program, the 2004 statistical correlation between the socioeconomics of a school (on a scale of 1 to 5, low to high) and that school's overall performance was reported to be .83. Correlations are reported on a scale from 0 (no relationship) to +/− 1 (perfect relationship). Clearly, a .8 indicates a very strong relationship between socioeconomics and achievement (Technical Design Group, 2005). This relationship is so strong that it is difficult for educators to keep cause and effect out of the thought process. Remember, as soon as we conclude that poverty is the cause of low scores, we have just disempowered ourselves as educators to make a difference in the lives of poor kids, and we ignore the evidence provided by the many "poor" kids who excel. We must constantly remind ourselves that while the strong relationship may exist, we refuse to give it meaning for the kids we teach, and we will do what is necessary to end that cycle of predictability.

Finally, the demographics of a school or district should never be used to "excuse" low or declining scores. It is important to recognize that although demographics will not stand in the way of providing a superior education to all students, they do contribute to scores, positively as well as negatively.

Physical Environment in Which the Tests Are Taken

The physical environment in which the students take a test can affect the entire testing population, positively or negatively. An attractive environment, of course, is desirable. Lighting, room temperature, and comfortable seating all play a part in how the students feel. Testing conditions should be as close to classroom conditions as possible. Hauling students into the cafeteria with a microphone and a proctor does not bode well from an environmental perspective.

If tests are inappropriately administered or if something out of the ordinary occurs, it affects all the students, not just one or two. Giving poor directions, not allowing the allotted time (if it is a timed test), or helping students who are obviously having trouble are all examples of conditions that adversely affect the accuracy of the scores. Then what if a lawn mower (or something equally distracting) is being used just outside the classroom during testing time? All of these distractions can have a disastrous effect on the overall test results from a school. Of course, most of these things can be easily controlled, but so often, they are not.

Attitudes of Teachers and Students Toward the Testing Program

High-stakes testing, in which results are printed in the newspapers and praise and indictments run rampant throughout a school community, is not a positive situation for educators. Some resentment is inevitable. Educators who are truly professional will never run from being held accountable for doing good work and producing significant results in students, but the history of large-scale testing suggests that results are often used to draw unwarranted conclusions. Thus, a positive attitude toward such testing programs must be built; it doesn't come automatically.

Occasionally, students are not motivated to do well on a standardized test. For many students, taking a test that "doesn't count for my grade" isn't accompanied by a thirst to excel. Negative or ambivalent attitudes toward a testing program may (and probably will) result in lower scores than if more positive attitudes had existed. The obvious goal is for teachers to support the high-stakes testing program (even if they may not agree with it) and for students to try their best.

Students' Test-Taking Skills

Test-taking skills enable students to get as high a score as they should, based upon knowledge, academic skills, and prior preparation. Contrary to popular opinion, test-taking skills are not intended to result in scores that are higher than those to which students' knowledge and academic skills entitle them. When students lack the skills to take a test effectively and efficiently, unless they are very lucky, they will score lower than they should. When large numbers of students in a school lack the skills to test well, this factor will certainly affect the group score, the one that is reported in the newspapers. It is important to understand that test-taking skills are not gimmicks; they are a set of skills that, when students possess them, will provide a more accurate assessment of the content being tested.

If the contribution of test-taking skills to test results is to be taken seriously, a schoolwide effort to build these skills is in order. These skills are not developed just to get higher scores on high-stakes exams. Test-taking skills will help students do well when they face really important exams such as those for college entrance, for professional licensing, and the like. These are the exams that will affect a student's life for a long time to come.

In a program that teaches students to take tests well, the skills that are necessary to build are first identified. Then teachers methodically work with students until they become comfortable with the test-taking experience. Students need to understand that the ability to take a test is something they will value, far beyond their formal schooling. Passing that required exam to become a teacher, doctor, lawyer, contractor, postal employee, or cosmetologist will be considerably more important to students than doing well on a state-mandated exam.

Curriculum Content and Test Content Alignment

Test alignment with the curriculum is never perfect, but it always matters. Assume that a school tests in Grades 1 through 6 in the content areas of language arts, math, science, and social science. Each time the school gives the exam, 24 group scores are reported (six grades times four content areas). When the content of the test is matched to the content of the curriculum, the "common ground" will differ among the 24 matches. That is, the amount of overlap will not be the same. Note the figures in the example on the following page.

Assume Case A in Figure 1.2 shows the overlap of program content and test content with Grade 4 science, and assume Case B to be that with Grade 6 science. With the overlap being much greater in Case B, and all else being equal, the probability is that Grade 6 students would score higher, relatively speaking, than Grade 4 students. The greater the overlap, the more likely the students will do well. When there is less overlap between program content

Figure 1.2   Curriculum Content and Test Content Alignment

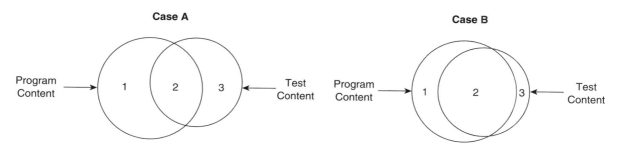

and test content, the students are being asked some questions that they really can't be expected to answer correctly. In Cases A and B, the less the area in portion 2, the less valid the test is for the students.

Program Quality

If we agree that program quality contributes to student achievement, and thus, to test scores, then we must define what we mean by the "quality of the educational program." If a definition eludes us, then how do we know what the quality of our program is? If this notion challenges your thinking, this book is for you.

A Very Important Point

High-stakes tests are administered for two reasons:

1. To understand more fully the degree of knowledge and skills of the students

2. To assist in evaluating the quality of our instructional programs

However, with an understanding of the six reasons just presented, we see how attributing the cause of test results solely to quality can easily be inaccurate.

Assume that a school has just received its reading scores. Further assume that the testing environment was poor, that the teachers' and students' attitudes toward the testing program were negative, that the students lacked good test-taking skills, and that some of the test content had yet to be covered when the students were assessed.

What is your prediction about the difference between the actual scores and what the scores might have been had these four variables been positive? The difference would likely be quite large. Yet these four variables, the ones that pulled the scores down, are unrelated to why the tests are given. None of these four is related to the ability of the students to read (which the test purports to measure), and none is related to the actual quality of the instructional program.

We see, then, that of the five variables over which a school has control (we cannot control a school's demographics), four have little to do with the reasons we test, and yet can seriously affect the scores. We label these four as "pollutants." Their presence "pollutes" the accuracy of the scores. The less the pollutants contribute to the scores, the more accurately the scores will portray the achievement level of the students (and the higher the scores will be).

So, when the quality of an instructional program is cited as the reason for less-than-satisfactory test scores, the "indictment" can be in error. This is not to say that the quality of the program is not a contributor to the scores. The program may be in dire straits. But using the scores in isolation to draw such a conclusion is wrong. Refer back to Step 3 of Concept 1 that suggests how to deal with this very real possibility.

CONCEPT 3: WHAT DATA ARE IMPORTANT AND WHAT DATA ARE USEFUL?

Beginning with *A Nation at Risk* (National Commission on Excellence in Education, 1983) and continuing with the No Child Left Behind Act (NCLB) and undoubtedly something yet unknown to follow, we educators have come under extreme scrutiny. The 1983 introduction to *A Nation at Risk* stated, "If an unfriendly foreign power had attempted to impose on America the mediocre educational performance that exists today, we might well have viewed it as an act of war" (p. 5). NCLB continues to apply the pressure today by imposing sanctions on those schools and districts that don't progress "satisfactorily."

For many years, the measures that have been used to pass judgment upon our profession have been test scores in some form or another. Norm-referenced tests in which students are tagged as "above" or "below" grade level are common. Performance-based or "authentic" assessments entered the arena at some point along the way. Currently, standards-based measures are getting the bulk of attention. "Criterion-referenced" is not an uncommon phrase. Regardless of how they are labeled, test scores, rightly or wrongly, provide the evidence of success or failure of our schools to our various publics.

Because test scores are the attention getter, and making or not making targets is the judge and jury for whether we are good at what we do, it is only natural for educators to focus on these measures. Questions like these dominate the scene: "How much improvement in the scores do we have to have?" "How many more kids have to move up a level or two?" "What can we do to raise those scores?"

In our effort to respond, we create school improvement plans *with the goal of raising test scores*. In the process, we slice and dice these scores in what seems an endless array of shapes and sizes. One of our favorite words has become "disaggregate." But isn't it natural to proceed in this fashion? After all, our reputations (and sometimes our jobs) are on the line. Doesn't it make sense to say, "Those scores have to go up, so let's focus on the scores"?

It may be natural, but it is a poor choice. The following section, "Importance vs. Utility," points out that there are data that are very important and there are data that are useful to help us improve, and often, they are not the same data. The section will point out the futility of only attending to test scores, while leaving the rest of the improvement picture to chance.

Importance Versus Utility

When discussing the various kinds of data related to education, sports analogies can often illustrate a point. The figure below contains four sets of information, A, B, C, and D. The information presented pertains to a professional basketball team. Look over the data and consider the following two questions:

1. Which set of data, A, B, C, or D, is the *most important to the team's stakeholders?* For a professional basketball team, the stakeholders would be the owners and the fans, because they are the parties to whom the team is accountable. Stakeholders are external to the organization.

2. Which set of data would be the *least useful to help the team improve?*

Basketball fans have fun answering these questions. Even for those who have little understanding of the game, the inquiry still works. In reality, answering the questions has little to do with the game and much more to do with the kind of information being considered.

A	B
1. Won 41; lost 39 2. Second place in the Western Division 3. Record away from home was 18 wins and 22 losses (league average was 13–27) 4. Team beaten in the second round of the playoffs	1. Team averaged 97 points per game (league average = 91) 2. Team gave up 95 points per game (league average = 93) 3. Team percentage shooting = 42.2 (league average = 46.1) 4. Team 3-point percentage shooting = 39.2 (league average = 34.5)
C	**D**
1. Team averaged 17 turnovers per game (league average = 15) 2. Team free throw percentage = 67.3 (league average = 75.2) 3. Team averaged 39 rebounds per game, 16 offensive, 23 defensive (league average = 42, 13 offensive; 29 defensive) 4. Team committed 40% of its fouls in the 4th quarter	1. Team practices 3 hours per day, 75% of which is on offense. 2. A basketball analyst on retainer states that 3 of the 5 starters have a questionable free throw shooting style. 3. In a 48-minute game, the five starters averaged 37, 42, 38, 35, and 35 minutes of play. 4. Preseason two-a-day practices last a shorter time than for most teams. 5. There is unrest among the reserves.

Repeating the questions with a bit more emphasis, of the four sets of information listed on page 11,

1. Which set is the *most important* to the team's stakeholders?

2. Which set would be the *least useful* to help the team *improve?*

The answer to question 1 is obvious: It is data set A. The stakeholders care about winning. They care about championships. They don't care how long their team practices or what their free throw percentage is, if the bottom line looks good.

Question 2 takes a little more thought, but I've done this exercise many times in seminars, and about three-fourths of a typical group will answer the question correctly. *The least useful set to help the team improve is data set A, the same set that is the most important to stakeholders.* What can you do with a win-loss record to help the team improve? Nothing! A win-loss record is a status report. Data set A tells you what *is,* and nothing more.

What we have just discovered is that in basketball, data that are the *most important* to the stakeholders are the *least useful* to the coach *to help the team improve.*

Now consider the sets of data that describe a school, using the same two questions (Incidentally, these data do not come from the same school. They are just sample statements.).

1. Which set is the *most important* to the stakeholders?

2. Which set is the *least useful to help improve* instructional programs?

A	B
1. 42% of our students met standards in reading compared to 54% statewide. 2. 54% of our students met standards in math. This is the same percentage as for the whole state. 3. The school scores ranked in the bottom half in the county in both reading and math. 4. When comparing our results to those schools whose demographics are similar, the school is in the top 20%.	1. 48% of the students currently have not mastered standard "A" in reading. 2. The main problem with the Grade 3 benchmark writing results is the lack of "organization." 3. On the district writing sample, 54 percent of the students achieved a satisfactory or better score. 4. 14% more girls than boys met standards in reading.
C	**D**
1. On average, 87% of the students attend class each day. 2. On four random days of checking, 57, 42, 60, and 56% completed their homework. 3. On the November benchmark tests in math, 62% of the students were "on target." 4. On the locally developed standards tests in October, 42% had met standards. In January, this figure was 58%. 5. 62% of the students indicate that they like school and are enthusiastic about the school as a learning environment.	1. 68% of the English teachers are implementing the language arts standards. 32% are not. 2. Grade 11 students write an average of two papers every three weeks (1–2 pages). 3. There are serious philosophical differences within the staff regarding the reading standards. 4. There is no organized curriculum for teaching writing. 5. 70% of teachers stated on the evaluation form that they felt ready to implement the math standards. 6. There is discontent among teachers with the manner in which planning occurred for the standards-based reading program.

The basketball data and the school data clearly mirror each other. Data set A in the school set consists of test scores and is the *most important to the stakeholders.* The stakeholders are those parties external to the school who pass judgment on school quality. As with the basketball data, *set A is also the least useful of the four* when it comes to providing interventions to improve the quality of instructional programs. Educators can do little with the knowledge that 42% of the kids met standards in reading, other than to say, "This percent needs to be higher." Test scores, as with win–loss records, are a status report. They tell us what is. They give no direction toward improvement.

For educators, there are data that are important and there are data that are useful. Sometimes they are the same data but more often, they are not. When a school staff does not distinguish between the two, importance will always dominate. That is, when I don't know the difference between important data and useful data, I am much more likely as a school leader to sit with my teachers, pondering the question, "What can we do to raise our test scores?" It's like the coach sitting around the table with his or her staff asking, "What can we do to win more games?" In both cases, we end up just guessing.

What, then, is the nature of those data that are the most useful? If test scores, as important as they are, do not provide us with the necessary information, what data will fill the bill? Concept 4 provides some answers.

CONCEPT 4: THE RELATIONSHIP BETWEEN THE QUALITY OF OUR WORK AND THE QUALITY OF STUDENT ACHIEVEMENT

When beleaguered educators are asked the question, "In this age of accountability, what are our stakeholders really asking for?" they are likely to answer, "Higher test scores. Our stakeholders want higher test scores." In a way, I suppose that is the right answer. But in reality, that's not what they want. *What they want is for us to be better at what we do. They want us to improve the quality of the programs that we provide to children.* They think they want higher test scores, but they don't. Test scores are just a conversation piece. They want high-quality schools with high-quality programs.

Most well-meaning stakeholders have the mistaken notion that test scores unequivocally report the quality of our schools and the programs in those schools. They typically believe that by knowing the test scores of a school, they can draw accurate conclusions about the quality of the work produced by the staff in that school. This is simply not true. Concept 2 pointed out that causes of test scores reside in six different places, only one of which is program quality. Quite likely, a school's test scores were caused by a combination of all six, to varying degrees. As was pointed out, if the four pollutants dominate the overall contribution to test scores, to conclude that the scores were unequivocally due to quality is obviously inaccurate.

Two Types of Data: Outcome and Process

When we make decisions about educational programs, two types of data that we use are *outcome* and *process*. Outcome data refer to student results, such as test scores, and process data provide information about the things we do in order that students will learn. Johnson (2002) calls this information "Policies and Practices" (p. 126).

Outcome Data

Outcome data have two major characteristics:

1. They report on the knowledge, skills, or attitudes of students: (1) what our students know, (2) what they are able to do, or (3) how they feel about learning.

2. They are quantifiable. They come equipped with numbers and are reportable. They refer to scores, percentages, and the like.

A plethora of outcome data exists on a campus. Included would be such information as attendance records, disciplinary referrals, number of books checked out at the library, homework completion rates, grade reports, and the list goes on. However, the piece of outcome data that gets the most attention outside of school is test scores, especially those that are considered "high stakes."

Process Data

Process information does not refer to students. Rather, it is information about the programs we provide to enhance student learning. The description of process information is expanded in Chapter 2, but for now, to keep it simple, let's divide process information into three categories. These are **M**aterials, **A**ctions, and **P**eople, or **MAP.** Process information reveals a MAP of what we do. Every instructional program on a campus has its own MAP. Reading, math, science, social science, fine arts, and physical education all have their own MAP. At the senior high school level, each course has its own MAP as well. We have an algebra MAP, a biology MAP, an English 10 MAP, and a physics MAP.

Materials (and equipment) refer to the quality, quantity, accessibility, and appropriateness of the instructional materials and equipment we use for a particular instructional program. Texts, supplementary materials, lab equipment, computers, and the like are in this category.

Actions are of two types, instructional and support. *Instructional actions* are those things that we do in the presence of kids. They include such effects as instructional strategies, grouping techniques, assessment activities, and reteaching strategies. *Support actions* are those things we do in the absence of kids. Curriculum planning, curriculum development, and staff development are the kinds of actions considered supportive. Also included in the actions category is the manner in which the available time is used in the classroom. How much actual instruction is occurring during the allotted time given to a content area?

People refers to the roles and responsibilities of the adults charged with making the instructional program succeed. Here we consider not only the roles and responsibilities, but also experiences, skill levels, and attitudes. The people category includes teachers, administrators, instructional assistants, specialists, and district office staff.

The Relationship Between Process and Outcome Information

How is the quality of process related to the quality of outcome? On one hand, we have the things we do (process); on the other, we have the level of student learning (outcome). I believe we would agree that when these two variables are the only considerations, they are highly related. As we progress through time, if the quality of our programs (process) improves, the quality of student achievement (outcome) will improve. Granted, there are other variables that can get in the way of this being absolute, but to stay focused, to accept this premise as true is an important step. Symbolically, it appears like this:

Process (P) $\longrightarrow$ Outcome (O)

We thus have established a major premise of educational planning: If we improve the quality of our programs, the quality of student outcomes will also improve.

It is important to decide just how much you believe this. When someone suggests this in a training room, we nod affirmatively. But do we believe it with passion, in our hearts? If we do, this belief will drive our behavior. To fit this premise into today's political paradigm, *"If we improve the quality of our instructional program, our test scores will improve."*

SUMMARY

Focusing too heavily on test scores, as this chapter has illustrated, is not useful because knowing the scores alone will not help improve the quality of our programs. They are very important, but more is needed to provide direction. When we only rely on scores as indicators of quality, we are missing a huge chunk of the data needed to improve. As Doug Reeves (2002) states

> Strategic leaders have the opportunity—and obligation—to place test scores in context. Indeed, they cannot use information to make strategic decisions if they only have test score data. They must also have information on the processes and practices that lead to those scores. (p. 136)

In this chapter, four concepts were presented to establish the limited utility of test scores in isolation. Important as test scores are, they do little to improve the quality of our work.

1. To place test scores in an appropriate context for program improvement, a structure or framework for doing the work of program improvement is necessary. A four-step process was suggested.

2. Test scores result from the impact of six variables: program quality, four pollutants, and demographics of the testing population. Only the last is beyond our control. The pollutants are those causal factors that have nothing to do with the quality of instruction, but can affect the scores a great deal. Acknowledging the pollutants' contribution provides a built-in caution about assuming too much from a school's or district's test scores. It also encourages educators to eliminate or to drastically reduce the presence of pollutants, as this will result not only in higher scores, but more accurate scores as well.

3. Data that are the most important to our stakeholders (test scores) are not useful by themselves when trying to improve the quality of our work. Answering questions about a set of basketball statistics helped us see this.

4. From day to day, from month to month, and from year to year, as the quality of our programs improves, the quality of student results will also improve. This provides a major premise for educational planning.

This fourth concept also provides the springboard for the remainder of this book. If we are to assess the quality of our work, then we must define what we mean by "quality." Success indicators must be identified, and then they must be measured.

THE BOOK: FROM THIS POINT ON

The "Dilemma of a Consultant," which began this book, alluded to an "aha"—that serendipitous moment in which I recognized the need to clarify and measure "quality." The remainder of this book suggests a definition of quality and provides tools to assist with its measurement.

Chapter 2 offers one definition of "the quality of an educational program." Labeled "The Three Faces of Quality," these dimensions are suggested: (1) quality of teachers, (2) quality of program elements, and (3) quality of leadership. It is emphasized that if any of these three "faces" is lacking, the instructional program will suffer.

Five tools to assist with monitoring and supporting the quality of these three are a part of Chapter 2. Tool 1 focuses on teacher effectiveness, and for any specified program, asks teachers to self-assess their knowledge and skills in 17 areas. These areas have been identified in research as a characteristic of an effective teacher. Tools 2 and 3 focus on the quality of 15 program elements tied to an instructional program. These elements are part of a program's MAP. Using these tools requires a high degree of dialog among teachers to flush out from among the 15 those dominant strengths and weaknesses of a program. Tool 4, related to leadership, introduces nine factors that define the health of an environment in which a program is being implemented. These nine factors are depicted in a profile that allows a school leader or leadership team to establish a prognosis as to the future success (or failure) of that program. Tool 5 asks us to recall the importance of effective collaboration (some would call it the "make or break" factor in successful school reform). A rubric with only two points, "Starting Out" and "Desired," identifies six major components of effective collaboration and asks a school leadership team to assess its current placement on a 4-point scale, with 1 equaling "starting out" and 4 equaling "desired."

In Chapter 3, two important elements that contribute to the quality of the "three faces" are identified—planning and capacity building. We plan . . . then we train . . . then we implement. If planning is effective and training is effective, we stand a far better chance of attaining high-quality implementation than if these two elements are carried out poorly. Tools 6 through 10 assist here.

Chapter 4 closes the book by challenging school leaders and their respective teams to consider the concepts presented herein, to decide just how much they agree with them, and then to address each of the 10 tools as to its potential on their own campuses. They are asked to determine which of the 10 would give "the biggest bang for the buck."

2

Defining the Quality of an Educational Program

THE THREE FACES OF QUALITY

SCENARIO 1

I'm sitting with a group of teachers and ask, "If you have a high-quality reading program on your campus (or math program or science program or . . .), what does that mean? What evidence would you look for in order to conclude that your reading program is one of high quality?" The teachers look at each other rather quizzically. Slowly they begin to offer their thoughts. "A high-quality reading program depends on good teachers. . . . These are teachers who really can connect with the kids. . . . They know how to teach. . . . They have a lot of tools at their disposal. If something doesn't work, they try something else. . . . They're very organized, knowing how to keep kids engaged with real learning activities, not just busywork. . . . They manage their classrooms well . . ." and the descriptions of quality continue, with varying characteristics of teachers being front and center.

By way of summary, after hearing their responses, I say, "What I hear you saying is that the quality of your reading program is based upon the quality of the teachers. Am I right?" They pretty much agree.

I'm with a group of teachers and ask the same questions, "If you have a high-quality reading program on your campus (or math program or science program or . . .), what does that mean? What evidence would you look for in order to conclude that your reading program is one of high quality?" As with Scenario 1, the teachers appear puzzled at first. Their thoughts slowly emerge. "A high-quality program is one that has a lot of effective instructional materials, for teachers as well as students. . . . The curriculum is solid. Sufficient time is given to fit all the content in. . . . Assessments fit the curriculum and provide teachers with important information. . . . The staff development program for teachers is strong. . . . There is strong teacher buy-in . . ." and the descriptions continue, with various parts of the program such as instructional materials, assessment, curriculum alignment, or staff development being front and center.

I respond with a summary: "What I hear you saying is that the quality of your reading program is based upon the various elements that comprise the program. Am I right?" As with the previous group, they agree.

Alert! The group from each scenario has agreed to a different set of descriptors under the same umbrella, "high-quality educational program."

A third group of teachers is asked the same questions as above, with the closing question being, "What evidence would you look for in order to conclude that your reading program is one of high quality?"

This group of teachers responds with the following: "A high-quality reading program requires a lot of support. The principal has to make it a priority, supporting it all along the way. . . . Teachers work together to provide the best program they can. . . . Assistance is continuously given. We're not just left alone to sink or swim. . . . We know what's expected and we're all on the same page . . ." and the responses continue, but this time focusing on various aspects of leadership that support a healthy environment or culture.

My comment to the third group is this: "What I hear you saying is that the quality of your reading program is based upon how school leadership has responded and how much support you have. I hear you say that a strong reading program occurs because of a supportive environment in which to work, brought about primarily by the principal. Am I right?" Again, there is agreement.

The three groups provided three different sets of indicators, all describing their perception of a "high-quality program." Which of the three scenarios produced the most accurate description or definition? A healthy three-way debate could ensue here, with each group arguing that theirs be considered the winner. "How can you have an effective program without effective teachers?" argues one. "But it takes much more than a group of good teachers," argues the second. "Good teachers will go wanting without adequate materials, time, a good curriculum, and additional support ingredients that accompany good work." "But," asserts the third, "in today's classrooms in which things are continuously changing, a healthy environment for implementing change, created by the building principal, must be present or the program will fall on its face. A strong leader who puts into place those things that create a healthy environment is essential!"

Which do you think is the winner? If you answered, "There is no winner. They are all essential in order for a program to be called high quality," then you are correct. The quality of any instructional program has three faces: (1) Effective teachers; (2) strong program ingredients; and (3) strong leadership support, leaders who assume the responsibility for creating a healthy environment in which instruction takes place.

Of course, there will be overlap. If I were to identify a particular element of program quality, I may argue that it fits into the "good teacher" dimension, while you may see it as a program ingredient. Where it fits is not important. What is important is that we begin to view the quality of our work as having a complex framework, fraught with potential barriers, but at the same time, very doable on every campus in this country, and it is the quality of our work that leads to student growth and achievement. When we elevate the quality of our work, our test scores will most certainly go up.

To reiterate, the test scores are certainly important. They are an essential part of the accountability paradigm. As a measure of students' knowledge and skills, a school's test scores are the bottom line. It is vital that each of us builds the skills to analyze scores and be able to take the results to a usable level. But if we attend to test scores at the expense of analyzing the quality of our work, we will have created a gap in our efforts to improve our programs that I don't believe can be filled. Therefore it is essential that we move into the arena of creating a structure for assessing the quality of implementation of our programs.

Figuratively, the "quality of implementation" schematic, as developed around the three scenarios above, looks like the figure below.

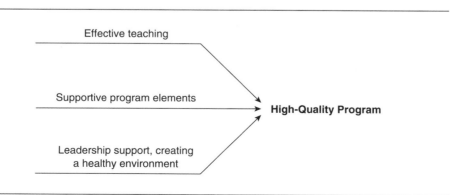

We can now view the development of the complete construct for defining the "Quality of an Educational Program." It proceeds as in the figure below.

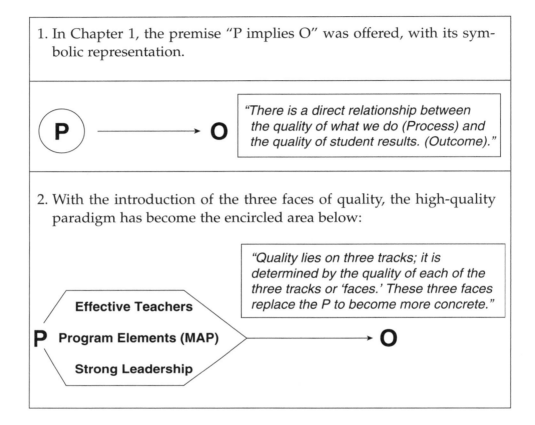

1. In Chapter 1, the premise "P implies O" was offered, with its symbolic representation.

"There is a direct relationship between the quality of what we do (Process) and the quality of student results. (Outcome)."

2. With the introduction of the three faces of quality, the high-quality paradigm has become the encircled area below:

"Quality lies on three tracks; it is determined by the quality of each of the three tracks or 'faces.' These three faces replace the P to become more concrete."

P — Effective Teachers / Program Elements (MAP) / Strong Leadership → O

ASSESSING THE THREE FACES OF QUALITY

The "three faces" structure shown above argues that an operational definition of a high-quality program is one that has effective teachers, plus a high-quality MAP (materials, actions, and people), plus strong leadership. It follows, then, that to provide a complete picture, in addition to collecting data related to student achievement, information regarding program quality must be collected as well. Discussion of each of the three faces follows, accompanied by a tool to assist in assessing that particular face of quality.

The First Face of Quality: Effective Teachers

What are the characteristics of an effective teacher? What set of criteria would you use if asked this question? Before we get too far into the discussion, allow me to set some parameters around the answers we give. The first face of quality describes those characteristics that enable a teacher to be effective in the classroom—alone, with the door closed! This face does not concern itself with aligning the curriculum or teaching to a set of standards or working well with other teachers or being a contributing staff member in planning meetings. We just want to know, "What makes a teacher effective with kids?"

There are multiple lists that I could offer to answer this question. Research on these characteristics has been a part of the educational scene for many years. Lists will vary in size and style; there is no one list to which we all ascribe, but there are some characteristics that most lists include. Resource B contains 14 such lists, and you will see more similarities than differences. Based on a thorough study of the lists, I have included in the figure below those that consistently appear.

Seventeen Characteristics of Effective Teachers	
1. Maintains high expectations for *all* students	10. Understands the students and their characteristics; can put the content into context in order to make meaning for the students
2. Has clear, focused, well-planned instructional lessons	11. Has a healthy sense of humor and carries this humor into the classroom in an appropriate manner
3. Is skilled in a *variety* of instructional strategies and has a solid knowledge of pedagogy	12. Has a system of incentives and rewards for students
4. Manages the classroom well; has discipline well in control	13. Has a grading system that reflects the goals of the course; system is fair in all respects
5. Creates a positive classroom environment; the classroom is a pleasant place in which to be	14. Has a system for monitoring student progress; uses the system as part of ongoing planning
6. Displays a caring, sensitive attitude toward the students	15. Uses a variety of assessment techniques; understands the importance of good assessment
7. Has "solid" base of content knowledge in those areas being taught	16. Self-evaluates and adjusts practices regularly; consistently tries to improve his/her practice
8. Is positive and enthusiastic about his/ her work; this transfers to the students	17. Is efficient in the use of classroom time. Students are consistently on task
9. Uses a different strategy from the original to reteach a concept that the students didn't understand	

The more "traditional" leader might look at the list, which certainly has face validity, and suggest, "This would be great to use to evaluate teachers!" The visionary educator, on the other hand, would view this list as a catalyst, providing a great opportunity to promote the need to actualize the goal of continuously trying to improve the quality of work in the classroom. *The provider of data relating to these characteristics, therefore, would be the teacher him- or herself.* To collect information in such a manner, Tool 1 is offered. A completed form is shown on page 25.

Notice on the completed form the funnel effect that surfaces. First, each teacher judges, without restriction, each skill as a plus or a minus. Comments are supplied when the teacher feels it is appropriate. Then, all the plusses and minuses are considered and reduced to lists of three. The question that the teacher then poses is, "How can I use my three greatest strengths to help elevate the quality of those areas I identified as my three greatest needs?" Plans for improvement can evolve from the results of this assessment.

It is important that teachers view this tool as reflecting *relative* strengths and needs, not as an evaluation tool to expose weaknesses. That way, the best teacher in a school will show three areas that need improvement and the weakest teacher will also have three. This is important in order that use of the tool does not equate to "evaluating," but rather to promoting continuous improvement in the classroom.

Tool 1 for duplication is provided in Resource A.

Sample of Completed "Analysis of My Teaching Characteristics"

TOOL 1: ANALYSIS OF MY TEACHING CHARACTERISTICS

Several elements of one's teaching can support or detract from the overall quality of the teaching process. Identifying these supports and deterrents will assist a teacher in deciding which areas to address in order to continuously improve.

Directions: Identify the instructional program in which the assessment is being made. Seventeen characteristics of effective teaching are listed down the left side. The "Description" column clarifies the characteristic. In the "Rating" column, record one of two symbols for each characteristic. The "Comments" column provides space to record anything the teacher wants to highlight. *Be sure you are addressing the program in question.*

A "+" indicates that the element currently supports the quality of my teaching.
A "–" indicates that the element currently is a deterrent to the quality of my teaching.
A "?" indicates uncertainty.

Instructional Program _____*Mathematics*_____

Characteristic	Description	Rating + or – or ?	Comments
Maintains high expectations for *all* students	Teacher behavior reflects the value that "All of my students will achieve. I expect it!" Distinguishes between high expectations and unreasonable standards. Expectations go well beyond grading. Does not have an unrealistic grading standard. This means *all* students.	+ 1	
Clear, focused, well-planned instructional lessons	Teacher is well-organized; planning focuses on the lesson to be learned; teacher makes certain that instructional materials are aligned with intended learning.	+ 2	
Teacher is skilled in a variety of instructional strategies and has a solid knowledge of pedagogy	Instruction is varied; not "sameolesameole" each day. Teacher understands how students learn and creates lessons to align with this understanding. Teaching is an art as well as a science, and this is reflected in what this teacher does.	– 3	
Manages the classroom well; has discipline well in control	Consistency, fairness, clarity, communication to students are all part of this characteristic.	+ 4	
Creates a positive classroom environment; the classroom is a pleasant place in which to be	Students look forward to coming to class. The class gets a "smiley face" without having a circus atmosphere. Students know they're here to learn, and the classroom environment invites learning.	+ 5	
Teacher displays a caring, sensitive attitude toward the students	Teacher has a positive view of the students; teacher is possibly one to whom students would turn if they were experiencing a personal problem; avoids strong criticism of students, especially in a group setting	+ 6	
Teacher has solid base of content knowledge in those areas being taught.	The teacher understands the content; teacher's knowledge goes well beyond what is being taught.	– 7	I am having difficulty with some of the current standards; could use help.
Teacher is positive and enthusiastic about his/her work; this transfers to the students.	This goes beyond just being a nice, caring person. This relates to the content itself. "I am enthusiastic about what I am teaching. I bring life to the content," is what this characteristic is about.	? 8	Re. the new math standards, not yet...but I'm trying.
Teacher uses a different strategy to reteach a concept that the students didn't understand.	When the teacher realizes that the students (or a student) have not understood, in his/her repertoire of strategies is a new way of looking at the issue. And if they don't get it again, perhaps there is a third way.	– 9	This is due to the issues identified above.

(Continued)

TOOL 1: ANALYSIS OF MY TEACHING CHARACTERISTICS (CONTINUED)

Instructional Program   *Mathematics*

Characteristic	Description	Rating + or – or ?	Comments
Teacher understands the students and their characteristics; can put the content into context in order to make meaning for the students.	Students have lives beyond school; they come from a variety of cultures and lifestyles. The teacher understands this. Lessons are geared to these differences, and practicality is a goal. Teaching is given a context.	– 10	I believe I will be able to do this when I have more confidence in my knowledge. Culture issues are not a problem.
Teacher has a healthy sense of humor and carries this humor into the classroom.	This sense of humor is part of #5 above. Humor is appropriate and contextual, often within the framework of the lesson.	+ 11	
Teacher has a system of incentives and rewards for students.	Rewards can be intrinsic or extrinsic. Rewards are purposeful and relate to the task at hand. Giving extra credit for bringing frogs to a Biology class or raising a grade for getting the most money for the jogathon does not fit here.	+ 12	
Teacher has a grading system that reflects the goals of the course; system is fair in all respects.	The teacher's grading system is communicated up front and continuously. Students always know why they got the grade they did on any assignment or at the end of any grading period. The grading system is never cast in stone.	+ 13	
Teacher has system for monitoring student progress; uses the system as part of ongoing planning.	Teacher rarely has to wonder whether the students understand a concept; continuous monitoring and checking for understanding is a part of the process . . . always!!	+ 14	I will be much better at this when my knowledge level improves.
Teacher uses a variety of assessment techniques; understands the importance of good assessment.	Does not depend on one or two types of assessments like homework and tests. Assessment is planned, never a last-minute rush job. Teacher understands the difference between good and poor assessments.	– 15	I know this is important, but to assess well, I need more confidence.
Teacher self-evaluates and adjusts practices regularly; consistently trying to improve is one of the teacher's goals.	Self-reflection is ongoing as the teacher assesses the quality of his/her work. Reflection can be micro (as in one lesson) or macro. Teacher owns failures; "blame" is not a part of the teacher's vocabulary.	+ 16	
Teacher is very efficient in the use of classroom time. Students are consistently on task.	Classroom runs like a well-oiled machine. Students create their own learning environments in which all are not necessarily doing the same thing, but all are in a learning mode. Minimum time is spent on things like checking attendance.	+ 17	

TOOL 1: ANALYSIS OF MY TEACHING CHARACTERISTICS

SETTING PRIORITIES

Directions: Record a + or – next to the 17 characteristics according to the teacher's assessment. Obtain these from the ratings above. Then identify the top three +'s and record them in the appropriate column below. Finally, rank the top three deterrents and place them in the blanks. A rank of "1" under the deterrent column represents the strongest deterrent; a "2" would be next; and so on.

1. _+_ High expectations for *all* students

2. _+_ Clear, focused, well-planned lessons

3. _–_ Skilled in a variety of instructional strategies; strong pedagogical knowledge

4. _+_ Manages classroom well; discipline is well controlled

5. _+_ Positive classroom environment; a pleasant place to be

6. _+_ A caring, sensitive attitude toward students

7. _–_ Solid base of content knowledge

8. _?_ Positive and enthusiastic about work

9. _–_ Uses different strategies to reteach a concept that the students didn't understand

10. _–_ Understands the students and their characteristics; puts lessons into context

11. _+_ Has a healthy sense of humor

12. _+_ Has a system of incentives and rewards

13. _+_ Has a grading system that reflects the goals of the course; fair in all respects

14. _+_ Has a system for monitoring student progress and uses it to plan

15. _–_ Uses a variety of assessment techniques; understands the importance of good assessment

16. _+_ Self evaluates and adjusts practices regularly; consistently trying to improve

17. _+_ Efficient in use of classroom time; students are consistently on task

Top Three Supports	Rank	Top Three Deterrents
#4 Manages classroom well	1st	#7 Solid base of content knowledge
#6 A caring, sensitive attitude toward students	2nd	#9 Different strategies to reteach a concept
#11 A healthy sense of humor	3rd	#15 A variety of assessment techniques

When the information collected from all teachers is displayed on the form shown on the next page, a vivid portrait of teachers' self-reflections appears. When the top three deterrents from each of the self-assessments are aggregated, profiles for improvement result, both for individual teachers and for the staff as a whole.

A common concern among school leaders might be that the "real needs" go undetected as "surface needs" reveal themselves. My response is first to acknowledge that possibility, but then to add, "If we want to create a culture of continuous improvement on a campus, we must encourage honest self-reflection. We may not get the answers we want initially, but as time passes and our efforts to create such a culture intensifies, we will."

Establishing a "Need" Matrix at a School

Characteristics of Effective Teachers	Teacher Self-Assessment: Improvement Targets						
	Teacher 1	Teacher 2	Teacher 3	Teacher 4	Teacher 5	Teacher 6	TOTAL
1. Maintains high expectations for *all* students				X		X	2
2. Clear, focused, well-planned instructional lessons							0
3. Skilled in a *variety* of instructional strategies and has a solid knowledge of pedagogy					X		1
4. Manages the classroom well; has discipline well in control		X					1
5. Creates a positive classroom environment; the classroom is a pleasant place in which to be							0
6. Displays a caring, sensitive attitude toward the students							0
7. Has solid base of content knowledge in those areas being taught	X		X		X	X	4
8. Positive and enthusiastic about his/her work; this transfers to the students							0
9. Uses a different strategy to reteach a concept that the students didn't understand	X						1
10. Understands the students and their characteristics; can put content into context in order to make meaning for the students							0
11. Has a healthy sense of humor and carries this humor into the classroom							0
12. Has a system of incentives and rewards for students		X					1
13. Has a grading system that reflects the goals of the course; grading system is fair in all respects			X				1
14. Has a system for monitoring student progress; uses the system as part of ongoing planning		X	X	X		X	4
15. Uses a variety of assessment techniques; understands the importance of good assessment	X			X	X		3
16. Self-evaluates and adjusts practices regularly; *consistently trying to improve* is one of the teacher's goals							0
17. Is very efficient in the use of classroom time. Students are consistently on task							0

The Second Face of Quality: Program Elements—Analyzing Our MAP

Three elements comprise the components of the second face of quality: (1) Materials (and equipment), (2) Actions, and (3) People. These were presented in Chapter 1. As noted, the three create the convenient and descriptive acronym, MAP. Every instructional program on a campus has its own MAP. A school has a reading MAP, math MAP, physical education MAP, business MAP, Title 1 MAP, the program for English language learners MAP, and the like. In high schools, each content area has its unique MAP: the algebra MAP, the physics MAP, the U.S. history MAP.

A Brief Review

Materials and Equipment. Here we are referring to the quality, quantity, accessibility, and appropriateness of materials. We are talking about materials and equipment for both teachers and students, and in some cases, for parents; we include both hardware and software. Basically, this aspect of a program's MAP covers the tangible elements.

Actions. Actions are of two types, instructional and support. Instructional actions are those that take place when kids are present, and support actions are those things we do when kids are not around. Instructional actions include such things as instructional strategies, grouping techniques, assessment, and reteaching strategies. Actions such as curriculum planning, curriculum development, or staff development are examples of those in the support category. Basically, the action portion of what I have labeled Program Elements refers to the things we do.

People. The people part of an instructional program's MAP directs itself to the roles and responsibilities of the adults involved in making the program work. These adults are the teachers, instructional assistants, instructional specialists, administrators, and district office staff. The people part of a program's MAP also deals with the extent to which effective work is done when all teachers are a single unit. This includes collaboration activities; the level of communication between and among staff, articulation from one grade level or course level to the next, and teachers' attitudes or receptivity toward a particular instructional program such as reading or social science.

If we were to figuratively take (1) all the materials, (2) all the actions, and (3) all the people involved in an instructional program and toss them in a barrel, mix them up, and pour them out, we would have the program elements, the second of the three faces of quality.

The Quality of Program Elements

All three components of an instructional MAP have "quality" attached to them. Consider the figure below. The vertical line on the left represents the quality of a program, from high to low. We call the horizontal arrow the "quality line," and it represents the overall quality, when all three components are taken into account. You might view the quality line as an average. Each "X" of the figure is one element, some aspect of the program's materials, actions, or people. The Xs above the quality line are those elements that are the stronger of the set. These are program "supports." Those below the quality line are the relatively weaker elements, providing a barrier to the overall quality. These are program "deterrents."

The premise is that we can improve the overall quality of the MAP by identifying the major deterrents and then work to strengthen them. For example, in a junior high math program, if the bottom three Xs encircled in the figure below were (1) instructional materials for low-achieving kids, (2) time spent in instruction, and (3) monitoring student progress, then part of our improvement plan would be to address these three elements.

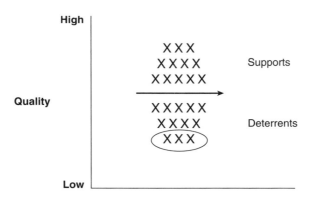

Once the "element" and "quality" concepts are understood, the next step is to answer the question, "What are those program elements that fit into the 'X' slots in the above figure?" For many years as a program evaluator, I collected information related to a variety of program elements. I made lists of elements, added some, and subtracted others, until I arrived at a set of elements that school staffs acknowledged were significant. Then I used these elements as part of a program evaluation. Not all the elements will be relevant for every program at every school, but using the list of 15 shown below will serve as a strong catalyst for analysis and discussion. Consider also that while there are certainly more than 15, it is important to work with a reasonable number. Few educators would choose to deal with a list of 40 elements. Fifteen has proven to be about right.

Fifteen Elements of an Instructional Program	
1. Materials and equipment for teachers	9. Organizing and operating the classroom
2. Materials and equipment for students	10. Physical facilities (library, classroom, labs, etc.)
3. Materials and equipment for parents	11. Teachers' collective knowledge and skills
4. Existing program content	12. Teachers' receptivity to the instructional program
5. Time spent on instruction	13. Collaboration among teachers
6. Teachers' schedules	14. Staff development
7. Diagnosing learning and prescribing instruction on a student or group basis	15. Communication systems
8. Assessing student results or outcomes	

Two tools, "Analysis of Our MAP—the Support/Deterrent Approach," and "Analysis of Our MAP—the Rubric Approach," are proposed to serve as a catalyst for dialog among staff when dissecting an instructional program. The tools use the 15 elements listed above and ask the participating staff, through discussion, to assess each element as a strength or relative weakness of the overall program. Accompanying the tools is a set of directions/suggestions for how best to conduct the activity.

I have heard success stories from many educators who chose to use the "Analysis of Our MAP" tools. I also have a personal story to share.

SCENARIO: PART 1

It was the mid-1980s. A high school on the West Coast achieved less-than-positive results on a high-stakes writing test. Staff scurried around in an effort to find a solution to the problem. The decision was made to implement a program in which writing regularly occurred in each classroom, regardless of content area. All teachers in the school were trained in how to do this, and writing commenced to be a part of each classroom's instructional program. Subsequent test results still failed to achieve the desired goal.

SCENARIO: PART II

In a positive, proactive environment, the school staff tried again. However, in this case, the elements of the school's writing MAP were assessed by staff, and supports and deterrents were identified. The results of this program diagnostic analysis were quite revealing:

The school had a veteran staff and a very stable staff. It was discovered that the median age of a very competent group of English teachers in the school (those primarily responsible for teaching writing) was between 45 and 50 years old. If an English teacher were somewhere around 45 years old in the mid-1980s, the chances were that he or she had never been trained to teach writing. Teaching writing as a process didn't surface as an instructional strategy until the late 1970s. Typically, teachers equated the *teaching* of writing with the *assignment* of writing: "Do you teach writing?" "Yes, I teach writing." "What do you do?" "Two papers a week."

An additional discovery was that no part of the curriculum supported the teaching of writing. The curriculum was a traditional one, focused largely on literature, grammar, and assigning compositions, with no direction for teaching students how to write well.

SAME SCENARIO: PART III

The conclusion could have been wrong with this assessment, but it wasn't. The assessment was correct. As a result, English teachers were trained and supported. Curriculum was developed. You know the rest of the story: Writing achievement, as measured by the important assessment, began to go up.

In this scenario, writing in every classroom was a solution unrelated to the cause of the problem. It may have had some benefit, but it didn't touch the real issue. When the deterrents were discovered, and plans were implemented to eliminate them, the quality of the program was enhanced, and the kids responded in kind.

Bottom line: Writing in every classroom was initiated as a means to improve test scores. Training teachers and developing curriculum were the proposed means to improve the quality of the instructional program. The school set out to improve test scores and it didn't work. Then they set out to improve the program, and the scores went up. There's quite a difference between those scenarios.

Unless educators are able to analyze the quality of a program's MAP, and to establish in their best judgment the dominant supports and deterrents, it is doubtful that substantive improvement will take place. As a profession we have become very solution focused: "We have a need. Let's try this!" We must discard that knee-jerk practice and become much more analytical regarding the strengths and weaknesses of the instructional programs we provide.

The completed Tools 2 and 3 shown on the following pages present how the results may have looked as the team progressed through "Scenario: Part II." The reader will note that closure for the activities resulted in targeted areas that the staff felt were causing the greatest difficulty.

Considerations When Using Tools 2 and 3: Analysis of Our MAP (AOM)

The purpose of these tools is to help a principal and staff or leadership team identify the relative strengths and weaknesses of any instructional program. The results of the process provide direction and help a group stay focused as they deal with various program improvement issues.

"Analysis of Our MAP," Tools 2 and 3, are not questionnaires. Don't put them in teachers' mailboxes with the directive, "Return by Thursday." The intention is that the forms be a catalyst for dialog, that they guide a group through the program's diagnostic process. A group of five to seven educators, teachers, and administrators come together to discuss an identified instructional program. To be a part of the group requires that members meet two criteria. First, each has a good knowledge of the program being addressed, and second, each member has a vested interest in the program.

The activity lasts up to one hour, *and it is timed.* Thus, from among the group, assign a facilitator and a timekeeper. The role of these two individuals is to keep the process moving and to avoid losing focus. "Off the subject" discussions really hurt the process. Also, and very important, the facilitator and timekeeper keep the group from moving into a solution mode. Because we educators are problem solvers (and typically not diagnosticians), we tend to solve too quickly, before we really have had a chance to look at all elements of the program.

Why have two tools that do the same thing? I have used both in my work, and different staffs prefer the two about equally. Take your choice. Tools 2 and 3 will each be presented separately, though they are intended to serve the same purpose. First, we will see a completed Tool 2, followed by instructions for use and helpful hints for using the tool successfully. Then, Tool 3 will be introduced with the same sequence of presentation.

Sample of Completed "AOM . . . The Support/Deterrent Approach"

TOOL 2: ANALYSIS OF OUR MAP— THE SUPPORT/DETERRENT APPROACH

Several elements of a school program can support or detract from the quality of the program. Identifying these elements will assist planners in deciding which areas to address in order to continuously improve. Completing this "Analysis of Our MAP" (Materials-Actions-People) as a collaborative exercise identifies these elements. Completing "Setting Priorities" as closure to the exercise identifies the elements that need attention.

Directions: Fifteen elements of a program are listed down the left side. Space to add two more is available on the back side. The "Description" column clarifies the component. In the "Rating" column, record one of three symbols for each program component. The "Comments" column provides space to record anything the group wants to highlight.

(1)   + indicates that the component currently supports the quality of the program.
(2)   − indicates that the component currently is a deterrent to the quality of the program.
(3)   0 indicates that the component is not appropriate or relevant to assess.

+ = Support
− = Deterrent
0 = Not assessed

Program being assessed   *Writing (Scenario 2)*

Program Elements	Description	Rating	Comments
Materials/equipment for teachers (consider quality, quantity, accessibility)	Consider those things *specifically* for teacher use, e.g., teacher text editions, curriculum guides, professional books and journals, technology equipment	+ 1	*Materials are there; we're not using them properly*
Materials/equipment for students (consider quality, quantity, accessibility)	These are items for student use; e.g., textbooks, supplemental books, technology, learning center equipment	+ 2	*same as above*
Materials/equipment for parents (consider quality, quantity, accessibility)	These are items specifically for parent use, e.g., kits for assisting students, materials for educating parents as to how to help students. Do not consider typical memos, newsletters, etc.	0 3	
Existing program content	Normally, this is in the form of curriculum standards; can be listed as instructional goals and objectives; also the content of the textbooks used	− 4	*We have no curriculum to support the teaching of writing*
Time spent on instruction (actual time spent teaching)	Consider only the time the teachers spend in direct contact with students. Is it understood and consistent across all teachers?	− 5	*We're not really teaching writing; we're assigning writing, but not teaching it*
Teachers' schedules (consider time for instruction, planning, duties, etc.)	Is there sufficient planning time? Reasonable duty time? Appropriate instructional time? Time to work together?	− 6	*This is not occurring in our writing program*
Diagnosing learning and prescribing instruction on a student or group basis	Relates to the process of identifying where students are and adjusting instruction to meet individual and group needs. May be formal or informal. Does a process exist? Is it positive? Does the process assist or burden the teachers?	− 7	*This is not done in writing*
Assessing student results or outcomes	Is there a system for assessing student progress? Is it efficient and effective? Consistent? Is assessment clearly connected to intended learnings? Efforts at performance-based assessment? Use of multiple measures? Do all teachers use and support the system?	0 8	*The assessment system seems irrelevant at this point, given other conditions*
Organizing and operating the classroom	Is the manner in which classrooms are maintained efficient and effective? Is the organization basically sound in light of the number of students? Do teachers discuss issues related to classroom management?	+ 9	

(Continued)

(Continued)

Program Elements	Description	Rating	Comments
Physical facilities (library, classrooms, labs, etc.)	Do the facilities support effective instruction? (This would be significant for science, P.E., and other areas in which the physical plant facilities play an important role.)	+ 10	
Teachers' collective knowledge and skills in the area being assessed	While some teachers will be stronger than others, when we look across all teachers, are the knowledge and skills, collectively, a support or deterrent?	– 11	*Most of us have not been trained in teaching writing*
Teachers' receptivity to the program	Do teachers agree with the intent of the program? Do they like the program? Is there an advocacy base for the program among the teachers?	– 12	*We basically have no program*
Collaboration among teachers	Do teachers meet regularly to discuss curriculum and instructional issues in the content area being assessed? Are skill building and coaching on the agendas?	0 13	*Again, with no program, this is not an issue; we don't currently meet together re.writing progress*
Staff development	Is there a strong link between staff development and what is planned for program implementation? Are staff development actions well received? Is there follow-through after formal workshop sessions?	– 14	*There has been none*
Communication systems (clear goals and expectations; understanding between principal, teachers, parents; articulation among the grades)	Do all levels within the school and community (especially the school) understand what is expected? Are lines of communication clear? Is it known who makes decisions and under what circumstances? Are there surprises? Is the situation fairly stable? What does curricular articulation among the grades look like?	– 15	*There is no such system for our writing program; current communication, generally, is good*

SETTING PRIORITIES

Program _____ *Writing (Scenario 2)* _____

Directions: Record a +, –, or 0 next to the 15 program elements according to the group's assessment. Obtain these from the ratings above. Then identify the top three +'s and record them in the appropriate column below. Finally, rank the top three deterrents and place them in the blanks. A rank of "1" under the "Deterrent" column represents the strongest deterrent; a "2" would be next; and so on.

1. _+_ Materials/equipment for teachers	6. _–_ Teachers' schedules	11. _+_ Teachers' knowledge/skills
2. _+_ Materials/equipment for students	7. _–_ Diagnosing learning & prescribing instruction	12. _–_ Teachers' receptivity
3. _0_ Materials/equipment for parents	8. _0_ Assessing student results	13. _0_ Collaboration
4. _–_ Existing program content	9. _+_ Organizing/operating the classroom	14. _–_ Staff development
5. _–_ Time spent on instruction	10. _+_ Physical facilities	15. _–_ Communication

Top Three Supports	Rank	Top Three Deterrents
Organizing/Operating the classroom	1st	*Teachers' knowledge and skills*
Materials for students	2nd	*Existing program content*
Materials for teachers	3rd	*Time spent on instruction*

Conducting the Activity: Tool 2

The group comes together, after having become familiar with the process, and sets out to "discover" the supports and deterrents of the program being reviewed. They address each of the elements in order. First is item 1, the materials and equipment for teachers. They discuss whether the materials and equipment for teachers are currently a strength or a deficiency. According to the simple rating system presented in the directions on the form, if the component is a support or a strength, place a (+) in the "Rating" column. If it is a deterrent, place a (–). A third option is to place a (0), indicating an irrelevant or uncertain issue. Some of the 15, though very few, may not be relevant for a particular program. For example, materials and equipment for parents (the third component listed) may produce a "0" when a high school staff is assessing its writing program, as was shown in the completed example.

The last column offers the opportunity to briefly comment about a component. It is important to comment if a particular rating produced a (–), because the group will want to document why that rating was given. Once in a while, hopefully not often, a rating of (+/–) will be given. This happens when the group cannot reach consensus for a particular component or when there are particular strengths and at the same time particular weaknesses that the group wishes to cite. When this occurs, definitely explain your rating in the comment column.

Owning the problem. Proceeding through the process, the team will address two delicate but critical elements. These are item 11, *teachers' collective knowledge and skills,* and item 12, *teachers' receptivity to the program.* These elements are sensitive ones because they ask the group to self-reflect and own up to possible deterrents of which they may be a part. For many, this is uncomfortable. However, it is essential that the elements be addressed. I don't believe many of us would disagree with the statement, *"Without self-reflection and ownership, school improvement will not occur."* If one is not willing to self-reflect, the result will automatically be denial and blame. An organization will never improve by blaming others for its condition.

Notice also on the second page of the form that there are two spaces for a school to add customized elements of their particular program to the list, if they deem them important. If this is done, that's fine. Just make sure that what is added is something over which the staff has control or can do something about. Adding an item to the list of 15 over which you have no control (e.g., student mobility), then giving that addition a minus, does little toward improving program quality.

Closure for the activity. When the group has completed assessing the 15, and there should be about 10 minutes or so left (the exercise may have gone a bit over the established one-hour limit), close the exercise in the following manner: Under the heading, "Setting Priorities," copy your ratings from the assessment just completed. There is no new work here. When that has been done, consider all the ratings and identify what you believe to be the top three supports and the top three deterrents and list them in rank order. This aspect of the exercise is critical because you are identifying those program elements that you will be addressing in an effort to improve the quality of your existing program. In the example presented regarding the writing program at a high school, identifying teachers' knowledge and skills and the absence of a writing curriculum led to significant improvement.

TOOL 3: ANALYSIS OF OUR MAP—THE RUBRIC

The setting and process for collecting the information using Tool 3 are the same as described above. The only difference is the format of the tool. Tool 3 uses a 4-point rubric to assess each of the 15 elements and then identifies the four most important areas to improve. Closure is reached when the team identifies which *one element* they believe would help improve the program the most. The same considerations and cautions should be applied to this rubric approach as to the support/deterrent approach above.

Tools 2 and 3 for duplication are provided in Resource A.

Sample of Completed "AOM—The Rubric Approach"

TOOL 3: ANALYSIS OF OUR MAP—THE RUBRIC APPROACH

Instructional Program ___*Writing*___

Several elements of a school program can support or detract from the quality of the program. Identifying these elements will assist planners in deciding which areas to address in order to continuously improve. Completing this Analysis of Our MAP (Materials-Actions-People) as a collaborative exercise identifies these elements. Completing "Setting Priorities" as closure to the exercise identifies the elements that need attention.

Directions: Fifteen elements of a program are listed down the left side. The "Description" column clarifies the component. For each component, the group will select which of four descriptions best fits that particular component. Place the number of the description in the "Rating" box. Leave blank those that are not part of the program (e.g., for some programs, the "materials and equipment for parents").

4 = This element is exceptionally strong. It could be described as in a category that is "above and beyond" what would normally be expected. Words that might come to mind when describing this component might be "exceptional," "excellent," or "exemplary."	3 = This element contributes to the overall quality of the program. While not among the strongest, it is seen as a positive factor. Improving this component would contribute to overall program improvement, but it is probably not a high-priority item. Words describing a component with this rating might be, "effective," "credible," or "meets expectations."	2 = This element has a history of mixed contribution to the overall quality of the program. While generally satisfactory, some parts can be strong while other parts are problematic. This one is really a mixed bag. Descriptive words might be "developing," "questionable," or "uncertain."	1 = This element is in trouble; its contribution is definitely in the negative category. Words or phrases accompanying this rating would be "disappointing," "inadequate," "well below what we would hope for." There is little question among staff that this component is in need of improvement.

Program Elements	Description	Rating
1. Materials/equipment for teachers (consider quality, quantity, accessibility)	Consider those things *specifically* for teacher use, e.g., teacher text editions, curriculum guides, professional books and journals, technology equipment	2
2. Materials/equipment for students (consider quality, quantity, accessibility)	These are items for student use; e.g., textbooks, supplemental books, technology, learning center equipment	3
3. Materials/equipment for parents (consider quality, quantity, accessibility)	These are items specifically for parent use, e.g., assistance kits for assisting students, materials for educating parents as to how to help students. Do not consider typical memos, newsletters, etc.	
4. Existing program content	Normally, this is in the form of curriculum standards; can be listed as instructional goals and objectives; also the content of the textbooks used	1
5. Time spent on instruction (actual time spent teaching)	Consider only the time the teachers spend in direct contact with students. Is it understood and consistent across all teachers?	2

(Continued)

Program Elements	Description	Rating
6. Teachers' schedules (consider time for instruction, planning, duties, etc.)	Is there sufficient planning time? Reasonable duty time? Appropriate instructional time? Time to work together?	2
7. Diagnosing learning and prescribing instruction on a student or group basis	Relates to the process of identifying where students are and adjusting instruction to meet individual and group needs. May be formal or informal. Does a process exist? Is it positive? Does the process assist or burden the teachers?	1
8. Assessing student results or outcomes	Is there a system for assessing student progress? Is it efficient and effective? Consistent? Is assessment clearly connected to intended learnings? Efforts at performance-based assessment? Use of multiple measures? Do all teachers use and support the system?	*We need one*
9. Organizing and operating the classroom	Is the manner in which classrooms are maintained efficient and effective? Is the organization basically sound in light of the number of students? Do teachers discuss issues related to classroom management?	4
10. Physical facilities (library; classrooms; labs, etc.)	Do the facilities support effective instruction? (This would be significant for science, P.E., and other areas in which the physical plant facilities play an important role.)	4
11. Teachers' collective knowledge and skills in the area being assessed.	While some teachers will be stronger than others, when we look across all teachers, are the knowledge and skills, collectively, a support or deterrent?	1
12. Teachers' receptivity to the program	Do teachers agree with the intent of the program? Do they like the program? Is there an advocacy base for the program among the teachers?	2
13. Collaboration among teachers	Do teachers meet regularly to discuss curriculum and instructional issues in the content area being assessed? Is skill building and coaching on the agendas?	2
14. Staff development	Is there a strong link between staff development and what is planned for program implementation? Are staff development actions well received? Is there follow-through after formal workshop sessions?	1
15. Communication systems (clear goals and expectations; understanding between principal, teachers, parents; articulation among the grades)	Do all levels within the school and community (especially the school) understand what is expected? Are lines of communication clear? Is it known who makes decisions and under what circumstances? Are there surprises? Is the situation fairly stable? What does curricular articulation among the grades look like?	2

SETTING PRIORITIES

Based upon your ratings, and the importance you attach to each of the elements (some elements will be more important than others), list the four elements whose improvement you believe would affect most the overall quality of the instructional program.

1. *Existing program content #4*	2. *Time spent on instruction #5*
3. *Teachers' knowledge and skills #11*	4. *Staff development #14*

If you were to pick just one for focusing your improvement, which would it be?   *Teachers' knowledge and skills #11*

Suggestions for Using the AOM Tools 2 and 3

Here are some suggestions to enhance the activity. These comments and suggestions have resulted from a considerable amount of experience using the two tools with leadership teams. Consider these, in no particular order of importance:

• Be patient. Trust the process. Remember, these are not questionnaires!

Diagnosing the strengths and weaknesses of a program with a structured process is not something we typically do. Therefore, while the exercise may look good on paper, it may not work very well the first time or two you try it. When talking to your staff about the intended use, my suggestion is to teach your teachers by using a relatively strong program in which teachers' knowledge and skills are a significant plus. I advise against starting with a troubled program in which teachers' skills are a weakness. Teachers don't need to feel like they're on the hot seat when learning something new.

• Make sure you are working with an ongoing program, not a program that has yet to be implemented.

Some teams have tried to use the form during the planning process, before the program becomes implemented; that has seen little success. It's impossible to assess something that isn't happening.

• Be sure to assign the facilitator and timekeeper roles; these two roles are what make the activity work. Guard against getting into a solution or "solve the problem" mode.

When using either option of the AOM, it is quite common for a group to have identified a "big ticket" problem, and then, rather than recording the rating on the form and moving on, to get into a solution discussion. When this happens, it dilutes the power of the diagnostic activity. Do not try to diagnose and solve a problem at the same time.

• With Tool 2, the support/deterrent approach, remember that all programs have supports and all programs have deterrents. The goal is not to obtain all (+)'s but to identify the relative plusses and minuses.

When you begin to use Tool 2, the staff, quite understandably, tends to treat it as an evaluation rather than a diagnostic activity. Thus, any minus is seen as some kind of blight upon the quality of the staff. Emphasize the word "relative" when assessing supports and deterrents.

• It is best not to have each group member fill out the form alone and then bring the ratings to the whole planning team.

To save time, sometimes this is done. I would advise against it. We want the ratings to surface as a result of group dialog and discussion in which ideas build on each other. When we bring our ratings to the table, the tendency is to build our own case so that we can be right, rather than making it a group decision.

- Do not use "language arts" as a program.

Language arts has too many parts for the exercise to work well. It includes reading, writing, speaking, listening, along with language mechanics, spelling, and so forth. Using language arts as a program for this activity will result in a less-than-satisfactory experience.

- Focus solely on the program being assessed. Don't allow the "halo effect" to take over.

According to Thorndike (1920, as cited on Wikipedia.com) a "halo effect" can occur when we associate one variable with another, even though they may not be connected (like eyeglasses being associated with intelligence). When involved in the AOM activity, we may assess one element because of our general feelings about the program rather than focusing on the element being addressed. A good example would be a competent staff giving itself a (+) because overall, they are very good, but failing to realize that for the specific program being assessed, collective staff knowledge and skills may really be a problem.

- Customize the form to fit your situation. But be certain to include only those elements over which you have control.

The two versions of the AOM are designed for a staff and its unique composition. You are welcome to change either tool any way you like, but to include elements over which you have little control (like monetary issues) reduces the impact of the exercise. When you do this, the message then becomes, "We have a significant program weakness over which we have no control that is preventing us from continuously improving. Therefore, we can't improve." We really don't want to send ourselves that message.

Hopefully, the AOM will not be seen as "just another thing to do," among the myriad of other things to do. Diagnosing a program's relative strengths and weaknesses before arriving at a solution is really changing the way we do business. Jumping to solutions without analyzing the program first is the "spray and pray" technique, to which most of us have become so accustomed.

The Third Face of Quality: Leadership and the Creation of a Healthy Environment

The third of the three faces of quality is leadership and support for creating a healthy environment for implementing an educational program, especially a new program. Because so many programs in today's schools are in various stages of "newness," this third face is crucial to attend to. It is important to remember that each content area has its own environmental health, even though the programs may be implemented on the same campus. Reading has its environment, as does math, physical education, and science, all on the same campus. A school leader will likely treat each content area on a campus in a different manner, perhaps emphasizing one while not paying as much attention to another. This can occur when political pressure has increased to improve achievement in areas like reading or math, with less focus, for example, on, say, science or social science. This differential may be unintended, but it is easy to see how it can occur. Of course, this unintended focus will result in a variety of implementation environments, some healthy and others not so healthy.

Before we get too far into this, we must distinguish between program environment and what we commonly refer to as school climate. School climate is generally described as the overall feeling tone of a school, using descriptors such as "positive," "toxic," "good," "poor," and the like. Within a school, however, a number of ecosystems may coexist. One school can have a healthy reading environment, an unhealthy science environment, and a toxic social science environment. In an elementary school, in which it is common for teachers to teach all or most content areas, we can have a healthy math environment, and with the same teachers, an unhealthy reading environment. The leadership "face" of quality definitely has an effect on a content area's environmental health.

Nine Factors That Define the Environment

Acknowledging that each content area has its own environmental health, a logical question surfaces: What factors define the environment?

My program evaluation experience suggests that nine factors define the environment in which a program is being implemented. For me, this list of nine has evolved over a number of years, and these factors have become key criteria when I evaluate any educational program. I discovered that these nine factors so dominate a program's environment and are so reflective of that program's leadership, that *they can be used to predict whether a program is likely to succeed, and the prediction will rarely miss.* But first, let's look at what those factors are, and then we will move to making predictions. Submitted in the form of questions, the factors are these:

1. Is there visible leadership support for the program?

2. Is there a visible advocacy base of well-respected teachers who support the effort?

3. Has the program been clearly defined?

4. Is implementation being monitored and supported?

5. Is there philosophical agreement among teachers regarding the program's intent?

6. Is there a specific set of standards and expectations for implementation?

7. Can the program, if new, be integrated with what we are already doing or is the program seen as a brand new venture?

8. Is there a payoff for implementers (generally teachers) to take part in the program?

9. Is the program relatively easy to implement?

A description of each of the nine follows. Before you begin your reading, think of a current instructional program with which you are involved—one that is less than two years old, if possible—and as you read, conduct an "in your head" assessment of how that factor is contributing to or detracting from the program's current environmental health.

1. Leadership support. We know from both our reading and personal experiences that any educational program on a campus requires visible support from its leaders, primarily the building principal. We acknowledge it, but do we really know how important it is? Do building leaders understand that if visible support for a program on campus is not seen by teachers that those same teachers will likely conclude that it's not all that important? How common are the two scenarios that follow?

A principal addresses the staff at a professional development session. The session is introducing standards-based mathematics, the latest of a long line of math programs that have begun and ended on this campus. "But this one is different," we hear, "This one will do it!" In addressing the staff, the principal states how important this session is, and how it is expected that the new standards-based math program will "really do it this time!" The speaker is introduced by the principal as a real leader in this "very important" mathematics endeavor, and the staff is admonished to "hold onto every word." Then, what does the principal do? He leaves! The last words the staff heard were, "I'm not the math expert!" If you were a staff member at this session, what would your feelings be?

This one is close to my heart (because I was the presenter). A high school principal invited me to speak to his staff about how to use test data effectively. Unlike the scenario above, he didn't leave the room. He was there the whole time—in the front row, reading the morning newspaper while I was speaking! It wasn't much of a session. His behavior gave the staff permission to mentally check out.

When incidents like these occur, the staff knows exactly how important that program is to the leader of the school: It's not! And the teachers will likely treat it as such.

Now imagine the same two scenarios, only this time the two principals actively participate, ask questions, move in and out of various groups, and basically take on the role of a learner. When the staff observes this behavior, the conclusion is that the principal is walking the talk. They will leave those sessions feeling very different from how they did after witnessing the scenes described above.

Does the leader have to be physically present every time there is a session of some kind dealing with the new program? No, that's impractical. The time simply isn't there. But because leadership support is such a critical issue when establishing a healthy environment, the leader *must consciously plan* how support for the program will be carried out. It doesn't happen by chance.

Remember, visible leadership support is proactive, not reactive, behavior. An astute principal plans what to do to evidence support; he or she doesn't just react when something comes up and then call it "support." A school staff needs to be able to answer, "Yes" to the question, "Does your principal agree with and support the instructional program?"

2. Teacher advocacy base. When an important educational program is in its initial stages, a small group of *well-respected* teachers on campus, strongly supporting the program and willing to be visible, is necessary to facilitate implementation. These teachers can influence others who question whether they should be doing this. All instructional programs need a cheerleading section. Without such a group of advocates, implementing a program successfully becomes a Herculean task. The district office can initiate a change. . . . The building principal can initiate a change. . . . But without an advocacy base of teachers, that change cannot be sustained.

If the principal is charged with getting a program off the ground, and there is no advocacy group on campus (the group need be only two or three teachers), the first step is not to try to implement the program schoolwide; the first step is to develop the advocacy group. Get someone on your side. Don't try to go it alone. Plan for how your advocacy base will be discovered and developed. Don't just pray that the group will magically appear—it won't. This is definitely a leadership "must."

3. Clearly defined program. When an important instructional program is being implemented, the principal should establish a "clarity goal" such as the following: "Every staff member involved with implementing the program will be able to carry on an articulate 10- to 15-minute conversation among themselves or with someone external to the school, explaining just what the program is." Issues such as how it is similar and how it is different from other programs, what a classroom will look like, what the students will do, what the teacher will do, and the like must be clear in the minds of every staff member. Clarity is an essential factor if a program's environment is to be healthy. Note the unfortunate example to follow.

Assume that implementing standards-based mathematics is a local mandate, replacing the traditional program that has existed for some time. As the building principal, you are charged with creating successful implementation on your campus. Teachers have participated in several capacity-building sessions. They have learned about the math standards, instructional strategies, how to use the new text, and the importance of assessing student progress. Then, someone inquires of a staff member, "Just what *is* a standards-based math program? How is it different from what you've been doing?" Your staff member is only able to respond with glittering generalities that basically say very little. What has happened is that important elements of standards-based math have been introduced, but in isolation. The teacher failed to see the big picture. The teacher knew the parts, but couldn't communicate the whole. This situation would be similar to a basketball player knowing how to dribble, knowing how to pass, knowing how to shoot, and knowing how to rebound, but not knowing how to play the game. As absurd as the situation would be for a basketball player, that is what occurs on many campuses when posed with implementing an instructional program. When overall clarity of the program is missing, problems surface, and these problems can be serious.

4. Monitoring program implementation. When teachers are charged with implementing an instructional program, trained to do so, then "licensed" to carry it out, they arrive at the proverbial fork in the road. That is, when the classroom door is closed, do they choose to use the program, or do they choose not to? In more than a few instances, planning occurs, capacity building occurs, but the program still is not implemented. Thus, the fourth factor, monitoring and supporting implementation, becomes an essential element of leadership and is a vital criterion in determining the health of the environment in which the program is being carried out.

Several years ago, I, along with several other educators throughout the country, was closely associated with a group of researchers from the University of Texas, headed up by Gene Hall, who was studying educational change. Hall and his team had developed a change management model known as The Concerns-Based Adoption Model, commonly known as CBAM. In several meetings with Hall and the CBAM team, I was struck by the emphasis that was given to monitoring the implementation of a program, what the implementers were doing, how they were feeling about the program, and the progress they were making. In a personal conversation I had with Gene, he stated that their research had shown that if an educational program is not being monitored and supported along the way, *it is unlikely the program even exists.* He went on to note that it may look good on paper, but it is doubtful anything of substance is happening.

The value of monitoring to support implementation is well supported (DuFour, 1998; McEwan, 2003). According to Fullan (1991), "Monitoring the process of change is just as important as measuring outcomes" (p. 86). DuFour (1998) makes a similar point in his book *Professional Learning Communities at Work* when commenting that inattention to monitoring a particular factor in a school indicates that that factor is less than essential.

Monitoring a program can be a double-edged sword. On one hand, it can be viewed by teachers as "checking up on us." Typically, this perception does little to promote effective implementation, at the same time contributing to an unhealthy environment, in which resistance and anger surface. On the other hand, monitoring can take on a "helping" role. When this occurs, creating a healthy environment is enhanced. Once an instructional leader acknowledges the importance of monitoring, how that monitoring is carried out deserves planning time.

5. Philosophical agreement. When teachers are asked to implement a new instructional program, one issue that they address, consciously or subconsciously, is whether they believe the new program is a good idea. "Does it fit with what I believe is philosophically sound?" is a question each will ask. Teachers don't have to necessarily agree with how a program is being carried out to philosophically agree with its intent. For example, as a teacher, I may not agree with the way standards-based mathematics is being implemented, but I do believe that standards-based math is a good idea. In that case, standards-based math will have passed the philosophical agreement screen.

Remember a few years ago when "authentic assessment" was the rage? Most of us agreed that educationally, this was a very sound practice. But it struggled and almost collapsed because it took too much work and too much time. We agreed philosophically with the proposed addition to assessment, but we disagreed with the manner in which it was being carried out. Still, authentic assessment would have passed this criterion.

What if we don't agree? What then? After all, "It's required! We're told we have to do it!" Educational leaders must include, as part of the school's implementation plan, the opportunity for teachers to express their philosophical concerns. Opportunities for healthy dialog about these issues, and how concerns can be allayed in the face of the requirement, will be provided by understanding leaders. Viable implementation strategies will be established. The reality is, mandates will not work unless those with differing opinions are recognized and offered the opportunity to discuss these differences. Discomfort on the part of the teachers will undoubtedly be the norm initially, but to attain a level of high-quality implementation, this discomfort must be acknowledged and managed well.

If a staff philosophically disagrees with a newly installed program, the environmental health of that program is in serious jeopardy.

6. Standards and expectations for implementation. Do teachers know precisely what it is they are being asked to do? In conversation, are they able to describe specifically what program implementation looks like, and can they explain what is expected of them to carry it out? When the answer to this question is "Yes," clarity has been established at the outset. When the answer is "Not really," confusion sets in. This factor is closely related to Factor 3, the clarity of program, but this factor deals directly with what teachers are expected to do. Confusion is an almost insurmountable barrier to successful program implementation and will certainly assist in creating an unhealthy environment. So often, teachers attend various forms of capacity-building/professional development sessions that explain issues, and talk about them, but somehow omit the part that says, "This is what program implementation in the classroom looks like, and what we all will be expected to do."

Tools 7 and 8, introduced later in Chapter 3, will strongly support this factor. They are the Essential Agreements and the Implementation Guide.

7. Integration of the "old" instructional program with the "new" one. Teachers have been around the block too many times, shouldering the burden of the latest fad, to initially take very seriously the next solution to education's ills. When being introduced to a newly designed program via a professional development session, teachers will view the presentation in one of three ways. Figuratively, this is how they will interpret what they understand the program to be:

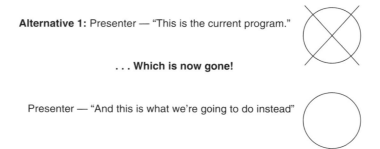

Alternative 1: Presenter — "This is the current program."

. . . Which is now gone!

Presenter — "And this is what we're going to do instead"

When teachers view a training session this way, they will immediately react, because the message they hear, regardless of the intentions of those responsible for the presentation, is "You've been doing it wrong!" Anger surfaces. Interestingly, an important capacity-building issue for leadership is not how wonderful the presentation was (articulate, well-organized, great materials), but rather what the teachers heard, how they received it. Too many times what teachers internalize, regardless of what is said, is this: "Our current program is no good; thus, you're no good!" This doesn't bode well for a healthy environment.

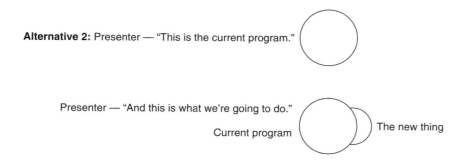

Alternative 2: Presenter — "This is the current program."

Presenter — "And this is what we're going to do."

Current program   The new thing

This is the add-on approach, and many teachers have no intention of adding something to their already overloaded curriculum. This is an especially sensitive issue with the current focus on curriculum standards. If teachers already view themselves as spending 100% of their time on the current program (maybe even 125%—overtime), why would they be eager to add more? My evaluation experience suggests that the typical response from teachers to this alternative is that of ambivalence. As soon as the teacher is once again behind closed doors, nothing is different from before. The program is gone (almost before it is started).

SCENARIO 1

Imagine the following. A unified school district brings teacher leaders, Grades 4–12, together to establish a set of benchmark assessments in mathematics and science (it could just as easily be language arts and/or history). The benchmark assessments are part of a long-range plan to implement and support a coherent, standards-based curriculum. The committee members have sound content expertise, they embrace the task, and the resulting product is impressive, and lengthy. Three benchmark assessments are identified or developed for each grade level and course. Blackline masters are produced, notebooks with directions compiled, and the material is distributed to teachers on the first day of school. This is where the happy story ends. Across the district, committee members are assailed with, "When am I supposed to do this?" "How do I fit this in with the tests I already give?" The benchmark assessments become a classic case of "adding on" without taking anything away. The teacher leaders who developed the assessments had several weeks to discuss, dissect, and warm to their task. They were proud of their product, but neither they nor the district curriculum staff had thought through the impact on those who had not had that opportunity.

Have you experienced this or something very much like Scenario 1? Most of us have, and some of us have been in all three roles at one time or another: curriculum specialist, teacher leader, resistant implementer.

That leaves us with the third alternative.

Note in the figure on the next page that the new program is inside and becomes part of the current one. Note also that as the "new thing," the benchmark assessments in our case, begins to grow (as shown by the dotted circle), we figuratively cut a hole in the bottom to let something out, the old assessment measures.

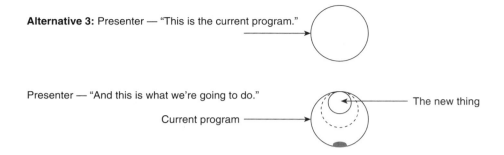

Alternative 3: Presenter — "This is the current program."

Presenter — "And this is what we're going to do."

Current program

The new thing

This is the "integrated approach," and *it is the one that has the best chance of getting a new program started halfway decently.* It is also the one that stands the best chance of creating a healthy environment for the new program to get a good start. It is important that teachers see a newly introduced instructional program as being "a part of what we're already doing." That way we start with the known, not with the unknown. Alternative 1 focuses on the new thing. Alternative 2 focuses on the new thing. Alternative 3 first emphasizes the current thing, and then fits the new one in. That makes quite a difference, and the instructional leader should pay attention to this difference.

SCENARIO 2

Same district, same task, same committee members as with Scenario 1. This time, however, the first order of business, directed by the curriculum specialists, is "How do we make this doable? We know you and your colleagues are already working as hard as you can and spending more time than we ask to make your math and science programs successful, but we also believe these common assessments will help. Is there a way to integrate the benchmarks within the existing programs, without adding more work?"

The resulting notebooks were still thick, but they were prefaced with two, single-page documents—the first, a letter from the committee members explaining the intent to integrate the new assessments, and the second, a "Then and Now" chart illustrating where, when, and how the new benchmarks could be used to replace existing tests and assignments. Result, nirvana? Not exactly; giving something up is still giving something up. The chances for a quality attempt at implementation, however, just improved immensely.

8. Payoff/benefit for implementers. When teachers implement a new program, it takes more time and more work, in a less comfortable environment than with the more established program. It is only natural that resistance results from this situation. Because of the natural inclination to resist new programs, part of a leader's role in creating a positive environment for implementation is to consider some form of payoff or benefit for the teachers (Hall & Hord, 2006; Harvey, 1990). "Why should I do this? What's in it for me?" are the teachers' questions that must be addressed. "Because I said so" or "Because the district (or the state or the 'feds') said so" is not a good answer.

Payoffs should be personal. One type of payoff doesn't fit all. For example, California's mentor teacher program a few years back paid each mentor up to $4,000 a year for his or her expertise. I have often suggested to a seminar group, "I'll bet you half of the mentors in your district would have done it for free," and the response is generally an affirmative nod of the head. The monetary amount was payoff for some but not for others. Getting more materials, a computer in the classroom, some time for collaboration, or the chance to attend conferences, might all be considered as forms of reward.

It may not appear at the outset that payoffs are possible to offer. Resources are limited. Your school may be overcrowded. There may be a lot of barriers to counter your attempts. But leaders should be aware of the need to try to establish some form of payoff, knowing that it contributes to the environmental health of that program.

9. Feasibility of implementation. From the outset, teachers must see a program as "doable." If I believe that I must give up on all of life to implement a newly designed program, I'm not going to do it. Most are willing to go "above and beyond" as a natural phenomenon of change. But most are *not* willing to go beyond what they consider reasonable.

When change is brought forward to a group of teachers, it is often introduced from the ideal state of implementation rather than from the initial stage. Thus, the change is viewed as too difficult and too demanding. It is far better at the outset to hear teachers saying, "I can do this," rather than "How do you expect us to accomplish this?"

A few years ago, a heavy emphasis was placed upon authentic or "performance" assessment. For most school sites, this was indeed an innovation worthy of consideration. It received support from many levels both inside and outside our profession. State testing programs began to include some form of authentic assessment in its array of measures. There was little problem with many of the factors identified in my list of nine: Leadership support was there. A strong advocacy base of teachers emerged (who wouldn't favor an alternative to bubbling an answer sheet?). Philosophical agreement was solid. But there was one small problem. The manner in which it was introduced on a typical campus and then attempted to be carried out was so time and energy consuming for teachers that a very well-intentioned reform almost died from its own weight. Here is one example: California in the early 1990s had a "hands-on" Grade 5 science test, a really good one, that required teachers to spend an inordinate amount of time setting up their classrooms for the exam. For most, authentic assessment passed quietly into the night, not because it wasn't a good idea, but because it just required too much time and effort.

These are the nine factors that a few pages back were introduced as defining the leadership role in creating a healthy environment in which the program is to occur. In assessing the health of an environment, the leader(s) will ask himself or herself the following:

"Am I showing leadership support?"

"Do we have an advocacy base of well-respected teachers?"

"What are we doing to ensure that the program is clearly defined?"

"Are we monitoring and supporting the implementation of the program?"

"Do we have philosophical agreement among staff?"

"What are we doing to ensure that our teachers have a set of standards and expectations for implementation?"

"Do our teachers see this program as a part of what we are already doing?"

"Do we have payoffs available for staff?"

"Is the program seen as feasible, or have we established an unreasonable set of expectations?"

The more yeses to the above questions, the more positive will be the environment for implementation, and the more successful the leader will have been.

TOOL 4: THE 9 FACTOR PROFILE

The nine factors above are the basis for Tool 4, "The Nine-Factor Profile." You will find the tool to be quite valuable to assess the environmental health of any educational program. Because understanding the profile and its potential utility is a bit more complex than for the previous tools, more time and space are committed to introducing and directing its use.

Once you are comfortable with the tool, you will be able to profile the presence or absence of each of the nine factors, and from the profile be able to predict with some assurance how successful the program is likely to be. The entire activity *takes no more than three or four minutes.* Here is how it works:

SCENARIO

A school is reviewing its relatively new standards-based mathematics program. Taking a few minutes, no more than three or four, the principal, sitting alone in the office, creates the profile shown on the next page. The profile is based upon how the principal thinks the teachers would complete it.

The principal then hands me, the consultant, the profile and asks, "What do you believe is the future of this program?" I know absolutely nothing about their standards-based math program, but I study the profile and then respond, saying something like the following:

"Your teachers believe that this program has been mandated, that they had little to say about what was to be done. This has created an uneasy feeling among the staff. More important, however, is that they're angry. They're angry because they believe they're being evaluated on something they don't understand. And they're frustrated, because there's no perceived benefit for doing what they're being asked to do. Although they have no qualms about the underlying concepts, they're possibly at the point of saying, 'forget it!' If your profile doesn't change, you're likely to lose the program."

I then ask the principal, "How close was I?" The principal responds, "You were right on. How'd you know that?"

How *did* I know that? The secret lies in first understanding the substance of the nine factors, and then being able to make predictions based upon how

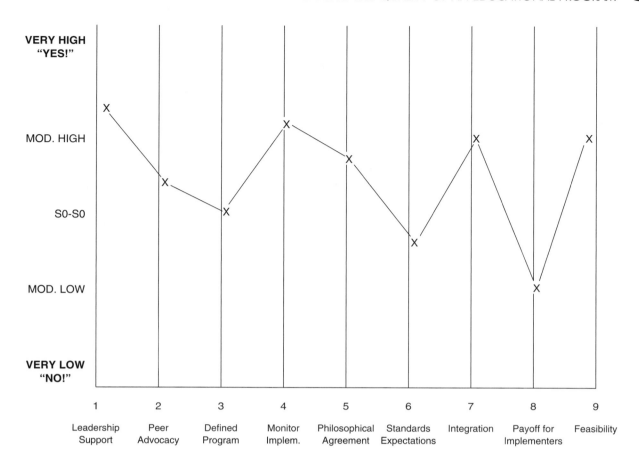

the various factors are positioned on the profile. For example, using the above profile, I first saw that leadership support, number 1, was rated high and that peer (teacher) advocacy, number 2, was rated quite a bit lower. When leadership support is high and the advocacy base is a rating level or so lower, the program may be seen by teachers as mandated, with their having had little to say about it. Think about it: When I as a teacher hear more from the principal (or other leader) about getting a program going than I do from the well-respected teachers on staff, it has "mandate" written all over it.

Furthermore, monitoring implementation, number 4, is relatively high, but clarity of program, number 3, and standards for implementation, number 6, are considerably lower. That's how I concluded that the teachers are angry. They are being checked on something they don't understand very well. Their having no qualms about the underlying concepts comes from the rating for philosophical agreement, number 5.

Put all that together and you have a failing program in the making.

Important note: It took three or four minutes to complete the profile. It took another few minutes for the principal to interpret it and draw conclusions. In less than 10 minutes, you have a relatively clear picture about the future success or failure of a program.

The profile and its interpretation do not carry a sophisticated set of research findings to support the contentions that I am making about its utility. However, the tool does have a lengthy experiential base in that I have used it successfully for several years. It also cannot be said to produce infallible results. Erroneous conclusions can be drawn, but it does not happen often. Conservatively speaking, nine of 10 profiles will produce an accurate picture of a program's environmental health.

Completing and Reading the Nine-Factor Profile

When completing the profile (see the figure on p. 53), the leader addresses the factors as if in the role of the implementers, typically teachers: (1) Does the leader believe the teachers see leadership support? If so, rate it relatively high. (2) Are well-respected teacher advocates visible? (3) Do teachers view the program as well-defined, and (4) do they sense that monitoring and support of implementation is occurring? Two of the last five factors in the list of nine are especially important to view through the eyes of the teachers. These are number 8, payoff for implementers, and number 9, feasibility of implementation. Be certain to mark the profile the way you believe the teachers see it. The leader may believe it is relatively easy to implement, but if the teachers believe it is not feasible, the profile must reflect this.

The key to reading the profile successfully is to look for relationships among the various factors. When two or three factors occupy a relative position on the scale, it suggests that a particular situation exists on a campus. The next two pages contain a list of suggestions regarding how to read a profile along with a rationale for each.

Suggestions for Reading the Profile

1. There are five vertical ratings on the scale from "Very High" to "Very Low." If leadership support is 1 to 1½ ratings higher than peer advocacy, it appears to teachers to be mandated. This is not a good start.

   Reason: If teachers view leadership as gung-ho, but that same enthusiasm is not shared by teachers whom they respect, it appears that leadership alone is pushing it; thus, it must be a mandate "from on high."

2. If leadership support (1) and peer advocacy (2) are "so-so" or below, bets are that very little is happening.

   Reason: When no one is viewed as championing a new instructional program, why change?

3. If leadership support (1) is relatively high and defined program (3), monitoring implementation (4), and/or standards and expectations (6) are "so-so" or below, confusion and irritation will surface among the teachers since they hear things but are confused about what they are hearing.

   Reason: Perceived leadership support, evidenced by a relatively high (1) rating, will be viewed by staff as "just another new program" if other aspects are rated low. When no one seems to be paying attention and there are no clear directions, "Why should we go out of our way?"

4. If leadership support (1) is at least 1½ ratings higher than philosophical agreement (5), it is definitely seen as a mandate. Resistance is likely to be high.

Reason: There is conflict in this situation because leadership is pushing it, and teachers don't believe in it. When teachers feel forced to do something that lacks conceptual agreement, resistance will build.

5. If defined program (3) and standards and expectations (6) are so-so or below, there's probably not much communication going on, and if it is, it's the kind that's unproductive. Teachers are pretty much on their own. There's undoubtedly considerable confusion. You're likely to lose the program.

    Reason: (3) and (6) are the clarity issues. When an intended program is unclear, it's hard to communicate anything but confusion.

6. If defined program (3) and/or standards and expectations (6) are so-so or below and monitoring implementation (4) is relatively higher, teachers are confused and angry. They believe they're being checked on or evaluated on something that's not clear. This is very unhealthy for your program.

    Reason: Being evaluated on something that is not clear in the first place is a good reason for anger, especially in this age of accountability.

7. If monitoring implementation (4) is so-so or below, it is highly likely that very little is going on, regardless of what the rest of the profile looks like.

    Reason: "If no one cares, why do it?" is the common teacher question. If teachers see a new instructional program as a "here we go again" effort, and the program is not being monitored and supported, little will change.

8. If payoff (8) is relatively low, with an otherwise fairly healthy profile, it may appear that all is well, but initial enthusiasm will die off, especially if feasibility (9) is also low.

    Reason: When teachers see that there is little in it for them, other than more work, a program will rapidly lose momentum. Implementing something new is hard work. Teachers need some way to say, "This is worth it."

9. If integration (7) and/or feasibility (9) are relatively low, especially when leadership support (1) is high, teachers are saying, "It's too much!" Resistance will continue to grow and you'll likely lose the program.

    Reason: If a program is viewed as overwhelming and the principal and district keep hammering on getting the job done, increased resistance is a natural fallout.

Try it out for practice. See how easy it is to do and how accurate your conclusions are:

1. Select an instructional program that is in its first two years. You might select your new reading, math, science, physical education, or fine arts program, for example.

2. Using the blank profile below, create a Nine-Factor Profile for the program. Be sure to mark how you believe the teachers would respond.

3. Pretend that you are an outsider reading the profile and that you know absolutely nothing about the program. Find which of the above nine suggestions fit your particular profile. Using those suggestions that match your profile, draw hypotheses about the program, using *only* what the statements say. *Do not bring your own opinion to the table.*

Compare the prognosis established by the nine suggestions above with what you believe about the program's future. Jot down your thoughts in the boxes provided under the profile. Are they the same? Different? They're the same, aren't they?

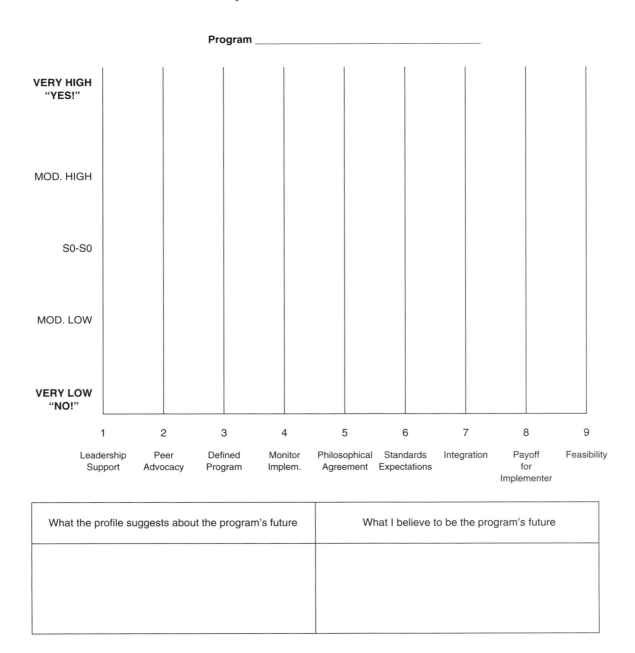

What the profile suggests about the program's future	What I believe to be the program's future

At first, when introduced to the profile, a principal or other educational leader might say something like, "This doesn't tell me anything I didn't already know. I know our teachers are frustrated; I know there is a lot of confusion; I know the program is difficult to implement." However, the profile reveals a realistic set of possibilities as to *why the conditions exist*. It is one thing to say, "The teachers are frustrated and angry." It is quite another to say, "The teachers are frustrated and angry quite possibly because the program lacks clarification and the teachers feel they are being evaluated on something they are confused about. In addition, it's quite possible that they don't agree with the philosophical underpinnings of the new program."

Extending the scenario, the principal then might say, "If we want to improve the environmental health of the program, we need to clear up the confusion and allow the teachers an opportunity to discuss the differences between the past and new programs. Perhaps a compromise can be reached. Apparently, monitoring the program, as well intentioned as it was, has sent the wrong message. We need to rethink how we support implementation."

AN ESSENTIAL ELEMENT OF ALL THREE FACES: EFFECTIVE COLLABORATION

Amid the pressures and challenges of today, and in the context of our ongoing pursuit of school improvement, the savvy educator knows he or she cannot do it alone. Evidence connecting teacher collaboration to improved student achievement is mounting (Educational Research Service, 2004). Reeves (2002) identifies collaboration as an enduring value in education.

Many years ago, when I was a classroom teacher, my high school had a staff of close to 70 teachers. We would say, "We have a staff of 70." Today, the need for collaboration is so crucial, I offer a different statement to seminar participants. No longer do we have a staff of 70, "We have a staff of one." When the staff is one, the Physical Education department assumes some responsibility for the students' achievement in Language Arts and the English department assumes some responsibility for the students' health and physical well-being. In an elementary school, the Grade 1 teachers assume some responsibility for Grade 6 reading achievement, and Grade 6 teachers respond in kind to the progress of the Grade 1 students. The collaboration goal is to become a *staff of one*.

Collaborative groups within a school vary according to purpose, with grade-level teams being typical among elementary staffs and subject or department-focused collaboration more common in secondary settings. My experience, and perhaps yours, supports this statement: Collaboration . . . does not happen by chance; it needs to be structured, taught, and learned (Garmston & Wellman, as cited in Educational Research Service, 2004, p. 3).

Throughout this book, tools are introduced that require collaboration, discussion, and shared resolve. This is most evident in analyzing our MAP, but the same can be said in examining teacher effectiveness and leadership support. Collaboration is a tenet and a practice that spans the three faces of quality, and like each face, effective collaboration has quality criteria of its own.

TOOL 5: A COLLABORATION RUBRIC

Tool 5 is designed to support improved collaborative processes. It is a rubric to assist in assessing the quality of collaborative practices on a campus. The major categories of the rubric are these:

Established philosophy ("Our staff is united around what we mean by collaboration. Ask any of us what 'collaboration' means, and we'll tell you.")

Leadership role of the principal ("Our principal is a positive force in leading the collaborative process. Time is allocated to do this work.")

Ownership ("We are in this thing together. Mutual trust and respect is the norm. There is no 'I' in 'team.'")

Nature of sharing ("We focus on the job at hand; we talk about student learning; the word 'blame' is not in our vocabulary, and we're through playing 'Ain't it awful?'")

Clarity of expectations ("All staff understand their roles and responsibilities; there is no confusion about the job at hand.")

Strategies ("We know there is no one correct way to collaborate; we work to get better at it.")

The rubric contains only two sets of descriptions for each of the six categories, "Starting Out" and "Desired." Description of the middle ground is left to the staff.

On the page following the rubric is a scale to assess the quality of each of the categories on a campus. The six categories are highly related to each other, so one would not expect large differences in ratings among them, but it is helpful to isolate each one, if for no other reason than to emphasize the importance of each.

An example of how an overall rating may look is shown on the graph. In this particular example, collaboration on this school site is beyond the beginning stages, with progress toward a healthy dialog and understanding leading the way.

	Desired	Starting Out
Established philosophy	We believe that ours is no longer a closed-door profession. We view collaboration as an essential resource for solving problems and elevating the quality of our work. We know we are better together than we are individually. Disagreement is healthy. We hold ourselves accountable for the learning of *all* students, not just those in our classroom. We believe that "celebration" should not be an uncommon word among us. We celebrate being a "staff of one."	Collaboration is not thought about as something requiring philosophical consideration. We work positively together on things like school plans, but will typically yield to lead teachers or to our principal when difficulty or disagreements occur. We're pretty much concerned about the achievement of our own kids in our classrooms, and see talking to others about their kids at best as "something interesting, but not about me."
Leadership/ role of principal	Our principal "walks the talk" regarding collaboration. Time is allocated for working together and is held "sacred." Leaders model collaborative strategies as the group consciously focuses on shared goals. District and school leaders are responsive to stated needs. Training and assistance are ongoing.	Our principal is helpful in arranging to get teachers together when something is to be accomplished, but his/her behavior does not communicate the essential nature of collaboration. There is no "marketing" or promotion of the advantages of the practice as "the way we do business."
Ownership	We are interdependent; collectively and independently we hold ourselves accountable for the quality of our work and for student results. It is "our success" or "our failure." We foster a culture of mutual trust and respect. All contributions are valued, as using the language of respect is a norm. Closed-door autonomy is a thing of the past.	We focus pretty much on our own classroom. Our profession in action is "my kids and I, in the classroom, all doing the best we can." When assuming responsibility for our work, we typically speak as an "I," not as a "we." Blaming or citing things beyond our control as reasons for some of our challenges is not necessarily the rule, but it is not uncommon.
Nature of sharing	Sharing focuses on common goals and mutual responsibility. When we come together, we talk about student learning, benchmark assessments, evidence of student learning, "at-risk" students, successful and unsuccessful strategies. The word "blame" is not in our vocabulary, and we have no pity parties.	Sharing almost seems a contrived activity. We do it, but to what end? To do something better or to get a job done? We do not resist it; we rather enjoy it. But it really isn't an integral part of our work on a continuous basis.
Clarity of expectations	Time for collaboration is carefully structured. All teachers understand their roles and responsibilities. There is no confusion about outcomes or "Why are we here?" We know that we are about shared planning, problem solving, new strategies, and interventions for at-risk students, in an ongoing way. This is the way we do business, even when no one's watching.	The description to the left in the "Desired" column is not uncommon for a single activity, such as when we write our school plan. But when left to our own natural m/o, we would not operate this way. The difference between "Desired" and "Starting Out," is that here, it is not the way we do business; it is not continuous when no one's watching.
Strategies	Our collaborative strategies are varied; we understand that there are several ways that collaboration can occur on a campus; we go well beyond "meeting and conferring." We may try teaming, coteaching, peer coaching, lesson study; in addition to collaborating about important student issues, we "collaborate about collaboration." We work to get better at it.	We don't consider collaboration as having strategies. Collaboration is coming together to discuss issues, perhaps to reach decisions of one kind or another, and then going our way. We would not view the examples included in the "Desired" column to the left as collaboration, and we would never think of behaving in this manner on our own.

Sample of Completed "Collaboration Profile"

Directions: Carefully read the descriptions provided for the "Starting Out" and "Desired" for eachcomponent. Create the profile that you believe best describes the degree of collaborative practicesat your site by placing a point on each of the six lines representing the six collaborative categories.By visually connecting the points, you will have established a "collaboration profile" from which toplan accordingly.

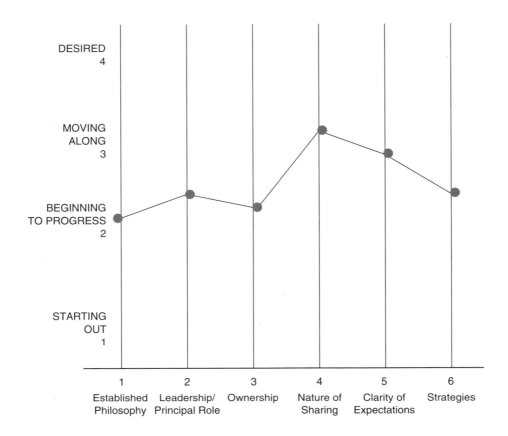

Overall assessment of our collaborative process and recommendations for next steps to continuously improve our process: Generally, we are beginning to progress; considering that we've only attempted to build a formal collaborative culture for three or four months, this is pretty good. We have higher-quality collaboration when we come together to get a job done. When we're working on day-to-day stuff, we tend to head back to our traditional comfort zone of doing it ourselves. There are no specific recommendations at this point other than to try to keep the importance of collaboration continuously in front of us, even when it doesn't seem natural.

SUMMARY

Chapter 1 introduced the premise of the direct relationship between the quality of an educational program and the quality of student results.

Chapter 2 has provided an operational definition of "quality." The phrase "the quality of an educational program" has become a cliché to the point that I believe the definition has been lost, if it was ever there.

Three dimensions or "faces" of quality were suggested: (1) quality of teachers, (2) quality of program elements, and (3) quality of leadership, which in this case translates to the health of the environment in which the program is being implemented. Tools to assist in the collection of information for each "face" were offered.

Teacher effectiveness in this context was described as those characteristics enabling a teacher to be effective in the classroom—alone with the students, door closed. The question posed was "What makes a teacher good with kids?" A list of 17 characteristics of effective teachers was presented and Tool 1, Analysis of My Teaching Characteristics, allows teachers to self-reflect about each of the 17 and identify those that are strong and those in need of improvement.

The quality of program elements, referred to as a program's MAP, was operationalized with 15 elements relating to the program's materials and equipment (M); the program's actions, both instructional and support (A); and the program's people, those responsible for making the program work (P). Tools 2 and 3 presented the 15 characteristics to a team of staff members and directed them to methodically identify the program's strengths and weaknesses.

The quality of leadership leading to the health of any program's environment can be determined by the presence or absence of nine factors. These factors, when collectively observed in a profile (dubbed the Nine-Factor Profile), were presented as an almost fail-safe way for an instructional leader to understand why a program is functioning the way it is.

Extending across the three "faces," and adding greatly to the quality of the three, is the extent to which a school staff has established a culture of collaboration. The chapter pointed out the importance of such a collaborative culture and offered a goal (and a challenge) to build a "staff of one" on each school site.

A collaboration rubric was offered as Tool 5 that assists with an ongoing assessment of how effective a school's collaborative practices are. Six components of effective collaboration comprised the rubric and "desired" and "starting out" descriptions were provided.

The primary goal of Chapter 2 was to operationalize the premise that the quality of an instructional program is directly related to the quality of student results. To do this requires an operational definition of "quality." Chapter 2 presented the "Three Faces of Quality." Effective teachers, an effective program MAP, and effective leadership result in a high-quality program, and the absence of any one "face" will deter progress. Tools 1 through 5 inform instructional leaders about the success of each "face" of a program.

3

Planning and Professional Development

A s an avid sports fan, I manage to watch a game or two on television each week. But all I see is the game as it plays out on the screen. From the first pitch, from the opening tip-off, from the kickoff, I watch the game. I see none of the preparation prior to the game itself. I miss the coaches' meetings; I miss the team meetings; I miss the practice sessions. I also miss the film sessions, and I miss all the instruction that the players receive from the coaches. To sum it up, I miss all the buildup. All I see is the *result* of the effort—the games. Rarely do I think about it, but when I do, I realize that the quality of the teams' performances is in large part due to the quality of what I did *not* see.

If I were an invisible observer of an educational program in progress, I would see the materials and equipment used; I would see what goes on in the classroom; and I would see the people at work—the teachers, administrators, and support staff. But I would not see the planning and collaborative efforts that went into the program prior to its implementation. I would not see the training that teachers and administrators received in preparation for putting the program in motion. What I would see is the program in operation—the "game"!

With each of the above two scenarios, it is obvious, even to the casual observer, that the quality of the performance during the game and the quality of performance in the classroom are related to the quality of the planning and capacity building that came before. If the pregame activities were of low quality, the quality of the game performance would likely follow in kind. Similarly, if the planning and professional development that occurred prior to implementing any educational program were less than effective, the "Three Faces of Quality" would undoubtedly have some wrinkles and be frowning.

Two important steps should be considered when any program is put in place, be it athletic or educational (or in business, if you prefer that comparison). They are planning and capacity building. Yes, effective teachers, effective program components, and supportive leadership encapsulate our definition of "quality," but the accompanying quality of these two pre-implementation steps will undoubtedly become relatively accurate predictors of the quality of the "three faces."

PLANNING AND CAPACITY BUILDING

Were these two steps, plus implementation, to be a linear process, the progression of activities would be something like this: "First we plan, then we build the capacity of the implementers, then we implement the program, and the 'three faces' take over." While linearity of this nature is rare in education, the three stages most commonly being done in tandem, we can nonetheless show the two, plus implementation, in this manner:

Planning ⟶ Capacity Building ⟶ Implementation

Based upon the first half of the book, if we look at the quality of three stages, the above figure would look like this:

Planning ⟶ Capacity Building ⟶ Effective Teachers

Effective MAP

Effective Leadership

While the "Three Faces of Quality" define or operationalize the overall quality of an educational program as it is being implemented, the supportive stages of planning and capacity building contribute in significant ways. It is difficult to conceive of a planning process being poor, yet yielding a high-quality program. Likewise, poor capacity building or professional development for teachers and administrators does not bode well for effective program quality.

Often, schools are required to implement a new program very quickly. Rarely is there the opportunity for a linear progression of planning and capacity building to be completed prior to implementation. That is the reason the "Three Faces of Quality" was the initial focus of this book. Getting to the heart of the matter right away was important for me as the writer. Similarly, it is essential that staff members of a school collectively say, "We know we are elevating the quality of our work when teachers' skills are improving, our program's MAP is becoming stronger, and the leadership of our school is consistently working to elevate the program's environmental health."

The importance of planning and capacity building cannot be overstated. They are critical to a program's success. While the definition of program quality lies with the effectiveness of our teachers, our MAP, and the program's environment, the quality of the two supportive stages will have much to say about the excellence of the overall program.

These two stages are so important that the second portion of this book has been dedicated to the part each plays in the overall picture. Several tools will be offered to assist with assuring that there is positive contribution during these preliminary phases of any program.

PLANNING

"Why is it that we never have enough time to plan but always have enough time to do it over?" Have you ever asked yourself that question? We all know that the planning stage in any endeavor is terribly important, but impatience so often gets in the way that we think we can save a little time by cutting corners. Never was there a better time than to revisit the old adage, "Go slow to go fast!" Bottom line: We have to plan well. It is essential.

Much has been written on the process of planning, but I will keep my focus to one specific issue, simple in concept, yet complex to pull it off well: That is, I will only deal with *the actual quality of the meetings when a team is seated around the table to decide how a particular program will become operational.* The emphasis is on the effectiveness and efficiency of those meetings.

Ensuring High-Quality Planning Meetings

We have all been a part of meetings called to address some aspect of program development. Some of these planning sessions were productive and moved us along very well. Others were unproductive and seemed a waste of time. What distinguished the successful from the unsuccessful sessions? What characteristics were present in the productive sessions that were absent in those that were less effective?

Fourteen contributors, the basis for Tool 6, tend to distinguish high-quality from low-quality planning sessions. These contributors, developed over my many years as a program evaluator, are categorized here under the broad headings of (1) Organization of the Planning Process; (2) Group Interaction; and (3) Supportive Elements.

Organization of the Planning Process

1. Planning-to-plan session: This is a meeting to discuss how planning will occur. Objectives, group processes, decision-making techniques, conflict resolution strategies, expected outcomes, and the like would be determined. This contributing factor is reserved for those instructional programs of a substantive nature for which several planning sessions would take place. Implementing a standards-based curriculum is an example. A planning-to-plan session occurs only once for any particular program, and there are no program decisions made during this time together.

2. Written norms: These refer to a set of established ground rules regarding how the group will operate when they are together.

3. Group facilitator: Identify a person to lead the planning process, and establish the facilitator's responsibilities.

4. Objectives for each session: Establish the expected outcomes before each session so the planning team knows what the purpose of that session is, what the expected outcomes are, and is aware of its roles and responsibilities.

5. Conflict resolution: Procedures for resolving differences of opinion are established ahead of time.

6. Decision making: Procedures are put in place to enable fair and consistent decision making. How decisions are made is determined ahead of time—e.g., majority rules, consensus, or a two-thirds vote.

7. Group members' roles and responsibilities: These are clear and understood by all group members, the degree of decision-making authority (empowerment) is known, and constraints are understood.

8. Materials available for reference: During each planning session, materials, including current data, are available for reference. This enhances the efficiency, and hence the effectiveness, of the planning sessions. (It eliminates the time wasted by running around looking for something during the time in which planning is taking place.)

9. Contribution of credible research to the plan: Known research findings are considered when formulating the plan; when strategies are posed, the group questions itself regarding the basis upon which these strategies were formulated.

Group Interaction

10. Group members' contribution: Each group member contributes positively, using the language of respect; the group holds itself responsible for obtaining input from everyone while a planning meeting is in progress.

11. Continual refocusing: An understood responsibility of everyone is to refocus when the group is getting off target (i.e., "bird walking").

12. Member domination: There is no domination by any group member or members; this is essential to an effective process. (When a group member dominates a planning session, the objective of the session rapidly changes from doing a good job to getting out of there!)

Supportive Elements

13. Time: There is sufficient time to plan, both on a short-term (one session) and a long-term (entire process) basis.

14. Availability of resources: Such aspects as released time, selected personnel, and access to materials are considered and made available according to the significance of the task.

In most situations, a list of 14 contributors requires more time and attention than a planning group is willing (or able) to give. If the group tries to attend to too many, we won't get the result that we want. Therefore, we reduce the number of items on the list to derive the intended benefit. My recommendation is that a staff identify which of the 14 planning contributors are *the most significant on their campus,* no more than five or six, and limit the list to those.

Tool 6 assists a staff in identifying the most important planning elements. Using the tool is simple and offers the opportunity for all members of the planning team to have a voice. But first, I offer a scenario that illustrates the probable outcome of using such a list.

Introduction to Tool 6: Checklist for Effective Planning

SCENARIO

A six-person team comes together to plan for the upcoming Standards-Based Mathematics Program in their district. The team realizes that planning for implementation must be of high quality if the program is to get a good start. Because time is at a premium, they want the best planning process possible with the least time spent. Having been given the list of 14 planning contributors, the team readies itself by first identifying which of the 14 it believes would be the most important given the makeup of the team and the school culture.

They go through the following steps:

1. Each member of the planning team completes Tool 6: Checklist for Effective Planning (see Resource A).

2. Members record their personal preferences on the tabulation sheet as shown below.

3. Each member then shares his or her selections, indicating why these choices were made and not others.

4. Discussion occurs regarding which of the contributors will be chosen by the group. Consensus is reached after about 20 minutes of discussion.

5. Group consensus is recorded in the column on the right of the table below. *This becomes the final list!*

Matrix of Important Characteristics of Effective Planning									
Contributors	**Rater 1**	**Rater 2**	**Rater 3**	**Rater 4**	**Rater 5**	**Rater 6**	**Rater 7**	**Rater 8**	**Consensus (Check those that will be used)**
1. Planning to Plan				X		X	X		
2. Written Norms									
3. Group Facilitator									
4. Objectives for Each Session	X	X		X	X	X			X
5. Conflict Resolution									
6. Decision Making		X	X						
7. Group Members' Roles	X	X	X		X	X			X
8. Reference Materials	X		X						
9. Contribution of Research	X	X		X	X	X			X
10. Group Members' Contribution	X	X	X	X	X	X			X
11. Continual Refocusing	X		X	X	X	X			X
12. No Member Domination		X	X		X				
13. Sufficient Time Given	X	X	X	X	X	X			X
14. Availability of Resources									

According to the chart, the six that were selected by consensus were these (numbers in parentheses denote where they appear as part of Tool 6):

1. (#4)—The objectives of session shall be written; expected outcomes for each session will be known ahead of time.

2. (#7)—The team's roles and responsibilities during the planning process are clear and understood by all group members; the degree of decision-making authority or empowerment is known; constraints are understood.

3. (#9)—Known research findings will be considered when formulating the program plan. When strategies are posed, the team will question itself regarding the basis upon which the strategies were formulated.

4. (#10)—There is positive contribution from each group member, using the language of respect; the group holds itself responsible for obtaining input from everyone.

5. (#11)—It is an understood responsibility of *all team members* to refocus when the group gets off target.

6. (#13)—Sufficient time will be allotted to plan, both on a short-term (one session) and a long-term (entire process) basis.

The facilitator of team meetings is a teacher-leader, although the principal is a member of the group. The principal made this decision, believing that all academic roles should be left at the door if planning is to be really successful. If the principal were the facilitator, group discussion would not be as spontaneous as is desired. The list of six planning contributors is printed nicely and placed on the wall.

At the first planning meeting, a short time is spent reviewing the list of six and clarifying any issues. The objectives of the first session are then distributed, clarified, and discussion proceeds. At first the group members are hesitant to assume the "traditional" role of the facilitator and redirect discussion that had gotten off track. However, about midway through the session, one member risks it, and the others affirm her, knowing that number 5 on the list, refocusing, was a responsibility of all members. The session goes relatively smoothly.

About 10 minutes or so before the session ends, the teacher-leader reminds the team that they need to evaluate the quality of the session. The point is made that no planning session shall end without assessing the quality of the meeting—not the quality of what was planned, but the quality of the session. The group addresses each of the six contributors, highlighting what went well and what could have gone better.

The meeting closes with the principal stating to the group, "I know I'm not the group facilitator, but I do want all of us to be able to say when we exit that door, 'Wow, that was a good session. We really got a lot done, and we had a good time doing it!'" Is there a better goal for any planning session?

When the above scenario plays out to completion, the following is likely to be the end result. I think you'll like what you read.

1.   The group will become a leaderless or self-managed team. This is exactly what you want to have happen. Each member of a leaderless team assumes responsibility for the success of the planning session. Number 11 from the list of 14 contributors, "continual refocusing," was selected by the planning group for inclusion on its abbreviated list. When a member of the group got off target, a member, not the facilitator, brought them back. Typically, we look to the facilitator or group leader to do that, but not here. Under this structure, everyone is responsible for themselves and everyone else living up to what was said would be done. Without such a standard, the group facilitator typically is the only one responsible for keeping the meeting on target. To extend the example, number 10 from the list of 14, "group members' contribution," was selected. It would not be uncommon for a group member other than the facilitator to say to another member, "We haven't heard from you for the last 20 minutes or so. Do you have a thought you'd like to contribute?" Again, because "group members' contribution" was chosen by the group as a desirable characteristic, a non-facilitating member feels comfortable responding in this manner.

2.   The quality of each planning session will be considerably better. Common sense tells us that high-quality planning, generated as a result of strong leadership, will yield a more satisfying product (e.g., a school plan) than if the planning process is questionable. What we want is for the planning team to leave every session saying, "That was really a good session." The goal of the planning process is to produce a high-quality plan, not just to get the thing done so we can run it up the flag pole to see if the boss salutes it.

3.   Your planning time will be cut by a significant amount. When you are focused, you save time. When the whole group sees its responsibility to stay focused, there is no wasted time!

Bottom line: When a staff has a set of criteria for conducting planning meetings and is aware of these criteria up front, then every member of the planning team assumes the responsibility for maintaining these criteria when a session is in progress. It is not just up to the group facilitator to make certain that the session goes well. It is up to everyone.

Remember: The criteria are always posted and always reviewed prior to each planning session.

Finally, an essential ingredient of high-quality planning is this: *The last 10 minutes of the session,* regardless of its length, are always reserved to assess how well the meeting went, using the established criteria. We evaluate the quality of the session by identifying what went well, what could have been better, how time may have been saved, and the like.

A copy of Tool 6 for reproduction can be found in Resource A.

Connecting Planning to Program Quality

The health of a program's environment, a product of strong leadership, was cited in Chapter 2 as a dominant contributor to that program's overall quality. The third face of quality focused on nine factors that defined the environmental health and was revealed in the Nine-Factor Profile. Success or failure of the program was noted as being closely associated with these nine factors.

Two of the nine, "clarity of program" and "standards and expectations for implementation," are key factors when reading and interpreting the profile and subsequently projecting a program's probable fate. When teachers clearly understand and can intelligently converse about a program and know precisely what is expected of them, it bodes well for the program's future success.

Tools 7 and 8, Essential Agreements and the Implementation Guide, are offered for consideration as the planning team designs a program for a district or a school. The two tools have potential for "raising the quality bar" considerably for any instructional program. While both tools are intended for initial development during the planning stage, they are intended to be fluid throughout the life of a program.

TOOL 7: ESSENTIAL AGREEMENTS

A planning team poses the question, "What are the things teachers should be doing to be fully implementing our new instructional program?" One way to answer the question is to establish a set of "essential agreements" for the program. Essential agreements are those elements of the program that must be carried out if that program is to be judged as implemented. These are program elements that initially are put into place to get that program off the ground. The initial design for this tool was established when I was part of a team at the California School Leadership Academy in 1992. We were designing a training module addressing program evaluation. Essential agreements were proposed as one means of assessing the extent to which a program was being implemented.

Essential agreements have three characteristics:

1. They are mutually agreed upon by teachers and school or district leadership.

2. They are few in number, no more than six to eight, and, in full, require no more than a page to describe.

3. They are explicit and observable.

When a set of essential agreements has been established, it becomes understood by all involved, teachers and administrators, that *not implementing the essential agreements equates to not implementing the program as designed.*

Here are some examples of how essential agreements read. These are obviously not from the same instructional program but rather cover a broad range of areas.

- Students will be involved in a variety of writing experiences, producing at least one written piece every three to four days.
- Math portfolios detailing academic progress will be kept for each student.
- Teachers will use a variety of measures to assess knowledge and skill acquisition.
- Students' ability to apply skills (extending beyond knowledge) will be assessed, and agreed-upon rubrics will be used for the assessment.
- In heterogeneously grouped classrooms, students will be homogeneously grouped for at least 25 minutes of daily reading instruction.
- Teachers will meet every two weeks to review, adjust, and support program implementation.

The last one referring to teachers' meeting was included to promote the notion that essential agreements can extend beyond the classroom.

Let's say that a school district (and thus, a school) has a set of essential agreements for a newly designed Standards-Based Mathematics Program. They read as indicated below.

Sample of Completed Set of "Essential Agreements"

Areas of Implementation	Essential Agreements: Grade 6 Mathematics
1. Instructional Time	Standards-based mathematics shall be taught a minimum of 1 hour per day.
2. Use of Materials	The XYZ instructional materials shall be the basis for math instruction.
3. Focus on Standards	All lessons shall be tied to one or more of the district standards, and standards will be posted prominently in the classroom.
4. Instructional Strategies	A variety of instructional techniques and grouping strategies shall be used in the classroom.
5. Assessment	Benchmark assessments shall be administered each quarter, and evidence shall be provided that these results are being used to affect instruction.
6. Collaboration	Teachers will meet monthly to share lessons, assessment results, and plan intervention strategies.

The six general areas from "Instructional Time" to "Collaboration" that were used in the above example help establish a comprehensive set of agreements and yet keep the number to a minimum. With these six statements, teachers know what is expected, a basis for the professional development necessary to launch the program is provided, and the principal and leadership team have criteria for determining whether the program is being implemented. Three important benefits rendered by one tool present a strong argument for its inclusion into an instructional program's arsenal.

Also, when the program is in its early stages of implementation, the information obtained by using essential agreements as a monitoring tool equips the leadership group to provide for appropriate interventions and additional staff development where needed.

Using the same six agreements, note the following results from a school. The Xs indicate the agreement has been met (three or four months following initial implementation).

Program Component	Teacher 1	Teacher 2	Teacher 3	Teacher 4	Teacher 5	Teacher 6	Teacher 7	Number Implementing Essential Agreements
Instructional Time	X	X	X	X	X	X	X	7
Use of Materials	X					X		2
Focus on Standards	X			X	X	X	X	5
Instructional Strategies	X	X				X		3
Assessment	X		X	X		X	X	5
Collaboration	X			X	X	X		4

Leadership now has a good grasp on "Where do we go from here?" Notice, also, that there is nothing in the essential agreements relating to the quality of implementation; they simply identify what is to be done. In addition, note that essential agreements can include program as well as classroom issues. In the above set, "teachers sharing lessons and assessments," under the heading of "Collaboration," is such an agreement.

To arrive at a set of essential agreements takes work and requires an open mind, a willingness to debate and compromise. But when the time is spent up front, much will be saved later on. Essential agreements really do operationalize the oft-spoken admonition, "Go slow to go fast!"

TOOL 8: THE IMPLEMENTATION GUIDE

The Implementation Guide is another easily understood and meaningful tool that can assist with establishing clarity and intent of a newly designed instructional program. I designed the framework for this tool during the initial days of my consulting work in the mid-1990s. Appearing as a 3-point rubric, its skeletal form looks like the one below.

Components	Ideal	Transitory	Just for Starters
Instructional Time	3	2	1
Use of XYZ Instructional Materials	3	2	1
Focus on Standards	3	2	1
Instructional Strategies	3	2	1
Assessment	3	2	1
Collaboration	3	2	1

To create the guide, first identify the important components of the program. These components might be likened to the Roman numerals I, II, III, IV, etc., when making a topical outline. As an example, assume these components to be (I) Time spent on instruction, (II) Use of the XYZ instructional materials, (III) Instructional strategies, (IV) Assessment, and (V) Collaboration.

Next, describe three levels of implementation for each component, the "Ideal," the "Transitory," and "Just for Starters." The three levels of implementation are listed across the top, and the components are down the left side. The descriptions are written in each cell.

A "3"-level implementation is labeled "Ideal," indicating the level that we would eventually like to see carried out by all teachers. A "1"-level implementation includes the expectations for implementation at the beginning. This "jumping off" level allows the teachers to become more comfortable with the new program, without having to fully implement immediately. A "2"-level is somewhere in between. In each of the 18 cells shown above, a brief set of statements is written (approximately 10 lines) describing how implementation in that cell looks. The figure on the following page illustrates how the implementation guide might read for a standards-based mathematics program.

The Implementation Guide provides a continuum of intent, from moving out of the starting blocks to the finish line. Initially getting our feet wet with "Just for Starters" implementation, moving to the "Transitory," and in a few months, arriving at the "Ideal" is the goal. With the implementation guide, a teacher can self-assess where he or she is for each component. Of course, we want all teachers at the "3" level for all elements, but a variety of configurations will occur. One teacher, for example, may be implementing at a 1-1-2-2-1-3 level (reading top to bottom for Teacher 1 below), while another may be at a 3-1-3-1-2-3 (Teacher 2 below). The recommendation is to not become overly analytical, but this form of assessing implementation has great potential for providing needed interventions.

Assume we have seven teachers implementing the Standards-Based Math Program. Each of the seven reports his or her degree of implementation using the guide, and the results look like the results below.

Program Component	Teacher 1	Teacher 2	Teacher 3	Teacher 4	Teacher 5	Teacher 6	Teacher 7
Instructional Time	1	3	1	3	3	3	3
Use of XYZ Materials	1	1	1	1	1	2	3
Focus on Standards	2	3	2	2	3	1	3
Instructional Strategies	2	1	1	3	3	2	3
Assessment	1	2	1	1	1	2	3
Collaboration	3	3	2	3	3	2	2

Assuming relative accuracy, much can be done with the above information to further the cause of program implementation. In the above example, use of the XYZ materials (five 1s, a 2, and a 3) and assessment (four 1s, two 2s, and a 3) are causing the most difficulty. Also, Teacher 3 appears to be lagging in implementation. Accurate self-reporting is key to the success of the guide. This, of course, requires a healthy environment in which teachers who are having trouble don't hesitate to say so.

Sample of Completed "Implementation Guide"
Standards-Based Mathematics Implementation Guide

Components	Ideal	Transitory	Just for Starters
Time Spent on Instruction	A minimum of 1 hour per day is spent but will exceed that if one or more important concepts have failed to reach closure. Evidence shows that this often occurs. 3	A minimum of 1 hour per day is spent but will exceed that if one or more important concepts have failed to reach closure. Evidence shows that this occurs on occasion. 2	A minimum of 1 hour per day is spent on the standards-based math program. 1
Use of Instructional Materials	All portions of the standards-based XYZ materials provide the basis for instruction. Using agreed-upon supplementary materials is common practice. 3	Including the remaining three parts is the goal, not yet fully realized. Using the agreed-upon supplementary materials to support instruction is beginning to be a part of materials usage. 2	The two most important parts of the five-part standards-based XYZ materials are in use. Familiarity with the other three parts is beginning to occur; using agreed-upon supplementary materials to support instruction is not common. 1
Use of Instructional Strategies	Multiple strategies are used regularly; close connections are made between the standards and the strategies employed; reteaching techniques, often different from those initially used, are a natural part of the instructional process; grouping for instruction is varied. 3	Progress is being made to extend the (1) variety of strategies, (2) reteaching techniques, and (3) grouping for instruction. The comfort level of teachers in working with these variables is expanding. 2	Different strategies are tried. Efforts are made to alter reteaching techniques from what was presented originally. Grouping for instruction is varied but less often and with less variety than with the other levels; teachers may not yet be comfortable with this. 1
Focus on Standards	During instruction, teachers explicitly connect each lesson with the appropriate standard(s). When asked, students can identify the standards they are learning. 3	The standard(s) for each lesson takes "center stage," and the teacher refers to the standard(s) frequently. Students referring to standards is not the norm, but it is beginning to happen more and more. 2	Grade-level standards are posted prominently in the classroom; lessons are standards based. At this point, most students are probably unaware that their lessons are tied to a standard. 1
Assessment	Assessments are tied directly to the standards; a variety of assessments is used, each having an appropriate connection to that particular standard(s). Data are used to inform instruction and establish "Where from here?" High-stakes test results (such as state testing) are considered in the whole of the assessment picture, but *do not* drive the process. 3	Tying assessments to standards is a natural part of the assessment picture. Focusing on using a variety of measures is an important element of the transitory level. The teacher is beginning to connect assessment results to "Where from here?" in the classroom. High-stakes measures are not an instructional issue. 2	Assessments are intuitively tied to the standards, but there is no formal connection; variety is not yet an issue—there may be some, but it's not a focus. Connecting assessments to standards is beginning to be done. Using the data to inform instruction and establish the "Where from here?" is in progress but more will be done. 1
Collaboration	Teachers meet regularly, formally and informally, regarding instructional and assessment practices. There is depth to the discussions. The teacher exchanges lessons and assessments with others. 3	Teacher meets regularly, formally and informally, with others regarding instructional and assessment practices. There is depth to the discussions. The teacher exchanges lessons and assessments with others. 2	Teacher meets regularly, formally and informally, with others about instructional and assessment practices. There is depth to discussions. The teacher exchanges lessons and assessments with others. 1

Creating an implementation guide is not a simple task, but neither is it horribly complex. Allowing four to six weeks to complete the task is normal, even expected.

To develop the guide, the following steps are recommended:

- Identify the components that will be placed down the left side of the guide. Do not go beyond six or seven. The maximum number of pages for a guide is two; one is better.
- Describe the ideal level of implementation for each element. When completed, scroll across all components in the "Ideal" column, and you will have described complete implementation (at that particular point in time).
- Create the "Just for Starters" column. This communicates to all that this level is the beginning and that a 1-1-1-1-1-1 level of implementation is completely acceptable at the outset.
- Describe the middle-ground level of implementation, "Transitory." This can be difficult to write, because implementation will progress at different rates with varying emphases within the teaching ranks. You may choose to leave that column blank and fill it in as implementation progresses.

Finally, the guide is never cast in stone. You may discover that something needs to be added, while at the same time, something else needs to be taken out or revised. Remember, the purpose is to clarify a newly designed instructional program and to establish a set of expectations for implementation.

A skeletal structure for The Implementation Guide is provided in Resource A.

TOOL 9: THE QUALITY AND DOABILITY OF THE PLAN

When charged with the task of planning, regardless of who requires it (local, state, federal, grantor), it is not unusual to create something that we think the "powers that be" want to hear. Because of this, we tend to put in too much. There is a down side to initially putting too much into a plan. First, when carefully analyzing the plan's content, we will no doubt discover it probably can't be done. There is too little time, there are too few resources, and there is too large a workload to be successful. Second, and in the long run the more serious of the two, little thought was likely given to whether the plan would actually improve the quality of what currently exists. In this case, we have created a plan to be *different*, not a plan to be *better*.

To prevent that from happening, Tool 9 is offered for consideration. It directs the planning team through a series of questions that reflect elements of the planned program, and asks the team to compare what is contained in the new plan to what is happening currently.

A completed Tool 9 is shown on the following page. To complete the form, proceed as follows. The process should take no longer than 30 minutes, and if it doesn't come out the way you had hoped, it will still be 30 minutes that were extremely well spent; improvements can then be put in place in a timely fashion (or you can trash the plan before it's too late).

1. Review the list of questions down the left side of the form to make certain that participants understand what is intended. If there is uncertainty, establish your own meaning.

2. Add additional questions that you would like in slots 15 and 16.

3. Discuss each question, hopefully with some depth to the conversation.

4. Mark the cell that best describes the group response. If any particular question is not an issue or is irrelevant, mark it in the far right column.

5. When completed, answer the two questions at the bottom of the form and determine next steps.

From the completed Tool 9 shown below, we see we have a potential problem. While perhaps not surprising at the initial stages, the current program was judged to be easier to implement and favored by the teachers. Using the tool, we see where some improvements might be necessary. Of course, if the tool had been kept at the planning team's side continuously throughout the planning process and used as a monitoring device, it wouldn't be needed when the planning process was completed. It would have already served its purpose.

Sample of Completed "The Quality and Doability of the Plan"

TOOL 9: THE QUALITY AND DOABILITY OF THE PLAN

Directions: For each of the questions, assess the degree to which the proposed program is better than the program currently being implemented. Place a check in the column of choice. When completed, answer the two questions at the bottom of the page.

Sometimes a proposed plan is an extension of what currently exists. If that is the case, assess how much the proposed plan adds to program quality. If for some reason a question is not relevant to ask, mark this in the last column.

Questions for Consideration	New Plan Much Better	New Plan Somewhat Better	No Real Difference	Current Program Somewhat Better	Current Program Much Better	Not a Relevant Question
1. When comparing the materials and equipment for teachers, which fares better?	x					
2. When comparing the materials and equipment for students, which fares better?		x				
3. When considering the relationship to our curriculum standards, which fares better?			x			
4. When considering the time that will be spent on instruction (the actual time teaching), which fares better?			x			
5. Considering the whole area of assessment (diagnosing deficiencies, assessing and monitoring student progress, final assessment), which program fares better?				x		
6. Which program fares better relative to planned staff development?	x					
7. Which program will the teachers prefer?				x		
8. Which of the two programs is the easiest to implement?				x		
9. Which of the two programs fosters opportunities for teacher collaboration?	x					
10. What is the assessment by the school principal of the quality of the two programs?			x			
11. Which of the two programs do the teacher leaders in the school prefer?		x				
12. Which of the two programs is easier to monitor and support the implementation of the program?		x				
13. Which of the two programs is clearer and more understandable to teachers?				x		
14. Which of the two programs will likely produce the higher level of student achievement?			x			
15.						
16.						

FROM OUR ANSWERS TO THE QUESTIONS, (1) IS IT PROBABLE THAT THE PROPOSED PLAN WILL PRODUCE A HIGHER-QUALITY PROGRAM THAN THAT CURRENTLY IN EXISTENCE? AND (2) KNOWING THE CONDITIONS OF OUR WORK SITE, IS THE PROPOSED PLAN FEASIBLE?

1. ___ YES!! ___ Yes ___ No _x_ Uncertain ___ NO!!
2. ___ YES!! _x_ Yes ___ No ___ Uncertain ___ NO!!

CAPACITY BUILDING

Capacity building here refers to any activity designed to improve the knowledge, skills, and practices of participants. These activities normally consist of a combination of training workshops and some kind of supportive follow-up. The goal is to build the capacity of the implementers—normally teachers, but also administrators—to implement what has been planned. We all know that building a base of knowledge and skills, plus developing an attitude to support implementation, is essential if success is to become a reality. Capacity building is the link between planning and implementation. If the *S.S. Capacity Building* ship sinks, so does the one following close behind—the *S.S. High-Quality Programs.*

Regarding follow-up, it is important, right from the start, to remind ourselves that capacity building is not limited to training sessions. Capacity building is not an isolated event. In addition to training sessions, the whole of capacity building is an ongoing process that includes high-quality planning and follow-up support in the form of ongoing coaching.

That reminder having been stated, however, this section, and its accompanying tool, do not deal with creating high-quality staff development programs. Much credible advice on that subject exists. Here, I am focusing on one very small piece, albeit a significant one: How do we evaluate capacity-building sessions that teachers attend, and what do we do with the results of such evaluations? I maintain that much important information is often lost when an inadequate process is used to evaluate capacity-building sessions. I'd like to suggest a change.

The evaluation forms that are used at the end of training sessions too often assess only the quality of the presenter (organized? dynamic? worthy of asking back?), plus, of course, whether the room was the right temperature and the goodies were satisfactory. Does the session warrant a "10" or only a "6"? The real intent of the training gets overlooked; i.e., *"Do those responsible for implementation have the knowledge, skills, and attitudes necessary to initially implement?"*

Whatever evaluation form a district or school uses for capacity building, that form must support the answering of this question. Knowing that you had a great presenter but that the room was too cold is nice information, but far nicer and more useful is knowing that 85% of the teachers understood the concepts presented and also found them to be valuable, but they do not yet feel ready to put them to use in the classroom.

TOOL 10: CAPACITY-BUILDING EVALUATION FORM

Consider using an evaluation form as formatted below. The objectives or intended outcomes of the session are posted on the wall or given as handouts with the training materials. Highlighted would be the knowledge and skills required for implementation that would be covered at that session. For each objective (shown as "1" and "2" down the left column in the figure), the participants respond to three issues: (1) the degree to which the participant understood what was presented, (2) the extent to which that objective had practical value for the participant, and (3) how ready the participant felt he or she was to implement that portion of content. For each outcome, the participant makes three checks, as shown. In the example below, for Outome/Objective 1, the trainee noted a high degree of understanding and relatively high personal value, but also indicated not being ready to implement. Look at Objective 2—Ouch! If large numbers of evaluation forms follow this pattern, some form of "redoing" is in order.

Outcomes/ Objectives	Degree of Understanding				Value to Me				Readiness for Implementation			
	High Degree ← → Low Degree				Very Valuable ← → Little Value				Ready ← → Not Ready			
	4	3	2	1	4	3	2	1	4	3	2	1
1	x					x					x	
2			x					x				x

The most important issue regarding evaluating capacity-building sessions is that data be collected to assess readiness to put the concepts into practice. Knowing this kind of information leads to more meaningful planning for future training efforts than if we did not have these data available.

A sample of a completed form is shown on the next page. If each member of a staff of 25 or 30 teachers submits this form at the end of a capacity-building session, the decision makers will have a far better grasp of the situation than if they only find out that the speaker was dynamic, the room was too cold, and the session was a 7.2 on a 10-point scale. If the form shown below represented the responses of a whole staff, the need for additional assistance with Objective 1, plus a whole redo of Objective 4 would be in order. It appears that, according to teachers' responses, they are ready to go with the content represented by Objective 3, but we can't expect too much right now regarding Objective 1 or 4.

Tool 10 may appear simplistic in light of the complexities of implementing a new instructional program. So much could have been said about the critical nature of capacity building, and yet I have chosen only to focus on how sessions are evaluated. Recall, however, that the results of our capacity-building efforts feed directly into the quality of program implementation. The "Three Faces of Quality" are affected by the

Sample of Completed Capacity-Building Evaluation Form

TOOL 10: CAPACITY-BUILDING EVALUATION FORM

Topic of Session _____*Implementing Standards-Based Math*_____ Date_____

Your Staff Category _____*Grade 5 Teacher*_____

The purpose of capacity-building sessions is to present information and strategies that will assist in change or new implementation. Input concerning these sessions is extremely important to future planning.

You will be provided with a list of outcomes/objectives that corresponds to the numbers listed on the left of the Rating Table. Please rate each on a scale from 4 to 1 according to the descriptors provided.

In each of the three categories on the Rating Table, place a check that best indicates your opinions. There will be three checks for each outcome/objective.

Rating Table

Outcomes/ Objectives	Degree of Understanding High Degree ← → Low Degree				Value to Me Very Valuable ← → Little Value				Readiness for Implementation Ready ← → Not Ready			
	4	3	2	1	4	3	2	1	4	3	2	1
1	x				x						x	
2		x			x					x		
3		x				x			x			
4			x				x					x
5												
6												
7												
8												

Comment:

The session was pretty good; however, far too little time was spent on Objective 4, Student Assessment. The materials provided didn't help either. Right now, don't expect me to do much of anything with assessment, not now anyway. I'm willing to give the other three areas a shot.

quality of training of the implementers. Teacher effectiveness in the classroom is affected. The quality of the program's MAP certainly is affected by the training the teachers and administrators receive. A poor capacity-building program will certainly affect the health of the program's environment. Review the nine factors and see just how much capacity building can affect them, especially (1) leadership support, (2) teacher advocacy, (3) clarity of program, (4) monitoring implementation, (5) philosophical agreement, (6) standards for implementation, (7) integration, (8) payoff for implementers, and (9) feasibility of implementation—that is, capacity building affects all of them.

I urge readers to review the evaluation form that is currently in use at your site. If that form does not directly address expected knowledge, skills, and implementation expectations, substitute Tool 10 or something like it. Don't miss out on this vital piece of information.

SUMMARY

The "Three Faces of Quality," introduced and expanded in the first half of this book, are the crux of the quality of any educational program. How can one argue with the significance of effective teachers, strong program components (MAP), and effective leadership resulting in a healthy program environment? Chapter 3 has taken a step or two backward and examined the precursors to quality implementation. While acknowledging that schooling and instructional improvement are seldom linear enterprises, this chapter has focused on two integral parts of program development: planning and capacity building. The premise is simple—planning and capacity building affect implementation. High-quality planning and capacity building greatly enhance the likelihood of high-quality implementation.

Five additional tools, Tools 6–10, were proposed to support planning and capacity building. I lobbied for including the tools as part of planning and training at a school or district site. Each of the tools is related to creating the highest-quality product possible. As always, the focus is on quality.

Tool 6, Checklist for Effective Planning, assists leadership team members to maximize the effectiveness of their planning meetings, save time, and otherwise focus on their goal. "Gosh, that was a good session. We got so much done. This program is really starting to take shape," are comments that should be the norm, not the exception.

Essential Agreements and/or the Implementation Guide, Tools 7 and 8, were introduced as part of planning, but their usefulness extends throughout the life of a program. These tools provide clarity for initial implementers and are valuable resources for monitoring implementation. As a result, use of these tools contributes substantially to a healthy implementation environment. These two tools are strongly recommended.

Tool 9, The Quality and Doability of the Plan, responds to the need to assess the quality and feasibility of a plan *before* it is put into action. This tool asks a planning team to do two things: (1) Compare the characteristics of a newly created program with that already in existence to judge whether, in fact, it is a better plan than what currently exists; and (2) determine if it is doable and whether we can pull it off. This tool can actually be used intermittently throughout implementation as a reminder of the initial intent and as a check on levels of support.

Capacity building (or professional development, if you prefer) was cited as the link between planning and implementation. An important consideration is that training sessions are not the beginning and end of capacity building. The point was made that often the purpose of capacity building (which is building the knowledge, skills, and attitudes necessary to implement the newly designed program) gets lost during the evaluation of these training sessions. Instead, evaluations too often collect information regarding the quality of the presenter. Thus, an important piece of information, relative readiness for implementation, is bypassed in favor of something far less important. Tool 10 is an evaluation form that not only collects information on the effectiveness of the session, but also elicits a self-report on the felt readiness to implement the content of a particular training session.

4

Setting Your Improvement Plan in Motion

You have progressed this far, hopefully because you see merit in the ideas presented, and because you see potential for using some of the tools. Dealing with high-stakes accountability is hard work, and a fresh approach can be enticing. Yet, realistically, there is too much content and there are too many tools in the whole package to consider using them all.

This closing chapter suggests some steps to decide which part of the book's content is worthy of immediate attention and what you would set aside for another day. *First,* identify those ideas that you believe are the most significant, the ones you do not want to forget. The ideas are listed below and you are asked to respond to each on a three-point scale.

STEP 1: ASSESS YOUR BELIEFS

Determine how strong your beliefs are, and how willing you are to respond to each concept below with some kind of action. Indicate the strength of your belief with a rating of 3, 2 or 1 as defined below.

3 = Strong belief and a commitment to act

2 = Believe that it is a good idea, but would hesitate to fully commit to doing something about it

1 = Would let this one pass

1. ____ Using the four steps to work with high stakes test results will keep us on target. See page 2.

2. ____ There are six reasons why test scores result the way they do, one of which we can't control, four of which pollute the scores, and only one of which relates to the quality of the instructional program. Addressing reasons why our scores resulted the way they did is an important step to take. See page 5.

3. ____ There is a direct relationship between the quality of an educational program and the quality of student results: As the quality of our work improves, the quality of student achievement will improve; as the quality of our work deteriorates, the quality of student achievement will go down. This message is important to continuously communicate. See page 15.

4. ____ A data-driven organization includes the formal collection of process information (relating to the quality of our work) in addition to the collection of outcome information (student achievement). This has been an issue throughout the book. See page 16.

5. ____ The quality of an instructional program can be defined by the "Three Faces of Quality." We will attend to the first face, teacher effectiveness. See page 22.

6. ____ The quality of an instructional program can be defined by the "Three Faces of Quality." We will attend to the second face, the quality of our MAP. See page 30.

7. ____ The quality of an instructional program can be defined by the "Three Faces of Quality." We will attend to the third face, the health of a program's environment. See page 42.

8. ____ We acknowledge that collaboration is extremely important. We will strive to create a collaborative culture on our campus. See page 57.

9. ____ Planning is an important element leading to a high-quality program. We will consider using the Checklist for Effective Planning to help elevate the quality of planning that occurs on our work site. See page 63.

10. ___ The notions of the Essential Agreements and the Implementation Guide are intriguing. We will consider the possibility of incorporating one of these into our efforts to clarify the standards and expectations for implementing a program. See page 71.

11. ___ Capacity building is an important element leading to a high-quality program. We will consider using the evaluation form to remind us that the purpose of capacity building is to build teachers' knowledge and skills so that implementation occurs. Our evaluation will address this. See page 80.

STEP 2: REVIEW THE 10 TOOLS

Quality Teaching

- Tool 1: Analysis of My Teaching Characteristics
  - This form identifies 17 characteristics of effective teaching. For a specific content area or course (e.g., reading, math, biology) teachers identify from among the 17 those elements that they believe are supporters of the quality of their teaching and those most in need of improvement for that selected instructional program. This is a diagnostic activity in which each teacher looks very carefully at each component and assesses the contribution of each for him or her. Results are intended to provide a picture of what improvements would keep teachers on the path toward continuous improvement. See page 25.

Quality Program

- Tool 2: Analysis of Our MAP—The Support/Deterrent Approach
  - This form and accompanying activity (scheduled for one hour and it is timed) identify 15 elements that comprise the quality of an instructional program and offer the opportunity for a group (5 to 7 participants) to identify those elements that they believe are most supportive of the quality of the program and which ones are deterring factors. This is a diagnostic activity in which the staff looks very carefully at the components of the program and assesses the contribution of each. See page 35.
- Tool 3: Analysis of Our MAP—The Rubric
  - This tool provides the same information as Tool 2, except that it uses a different format. The same 15 elements of an effective program are considered, and rather than a support/deterrent choice, the group of 5 to 7 people uses a four-point rubric, placing each element on the scale. The exercise culminates in the group's choosing which 4 of the 15 have the greatest need for improvement, and then which one element has the highest need. See page 38.

Quality Leadership

- Tool 4: The Nine-Factor Profile
  - This tool assists the principal in establishing a prognosis for the success of any educational program. On a scale from very high to very low, the principal creates a profile, using the nine factors, that describes the health of the environment in which a program is being implemented. See page 52.
- Tool 5: A Collaboration Rubric
  - Six characteristics of effective collaboration are provided, with accompanying descriptions of "Desired," and "Starting Out." Each

characteristic is placed on a four-point scale indicating the degree to which that characteristic is present on the campus. A composite of the six creates a collaboration profile that can be used to assess the quality of the overall collaborative effort. See page 58.

Quality Planning

- Tool 6: Checklist for Effective Planning
  - This tool identifies 14 characteristics of an effective planning session. The planning team identifies which of the characteristics it will focus on (5 to 8) and ensures that these are always present when the team comes together. The last 10 minutes of any planning session are used to evaluate the effectiveness of the session, using the selected characteristics. See page 108 or 67.
- Tool 7: Essential Agreements
  - This tool involves a set of six to eight statements that teachers and leaders agree must be accomplished for an intended change to be considered "implemented." The agreements meet three criteria: They are (1) agreed upon by teachers and leadership, (2) few in number, and (3) observable. Teachers know up front that if they are not implementing the essential agreements, they are not implementing the program. See page 71.
- Tool 8: The Implementation Guide
  - This tool provides an outline that describes the implementation of an instructional program in three stages: (1) Ideal; (2) Transitory; (3) Just for Starters. These stages are described in a matrix in which the major components of a program are identified (e.g., use of instructional materials, instructional strategies, grouping for instruction, assessment techniques, collaboration). With the Implementation Guide, it is possible to identify the level of implementation for individual teachers and for a staff. See page 74.
- Tool 9: The Quality and Doability of the Plan
  - This tool offers 14 questions that compare the proposed plan to the program currently in place. Assessments are made as to whether the new is preferable to the old. The final question asks the staff to project whether the new program will be of a higher quality than the one currently in existence. See page 77.

Quality Capacity Building

- Tool 10: Capacity-Building Evaluation Form
  - This tool identifies the intended outcomes of a staff development session and assesses each outcome in three areas: (1) degree of understanding, (2) personal value to the participant, and (3) readiness for implementation. Information from this form will assist with identifying next steps for professional development. See page 80.

STEP 3: DETERMINE HOW YOU WILL USE THE TOOLS

	Does it fit with our beliefs?	Would it work on our site?	What difficulties might we encounter when using this tool?
Tool 1: Analysis of My Teaching Characteristics			
Tool 2: Analysis of Our MAP—The Support/ Deterrent Approach			
Tool 3: Analysis of Our MAP—The Rubric Approach			
Tool 4: The Nine-Factor Profile			
Tool 5: A Collaboration Rubric			
Tool 6: Checklist for Effective Planning			
Tool 7: Essential Agreements			
Tool 8: The Implementation Guide			
Tool 9: The Quality and Doability of the Plan			
Tool 10: Capacity-Building Evaluation Form			

Considering time, energy, resources, needs on your campus, and makeup of staff, which tools do you feel would give you the "biggest bang for your buck," relative to improving the quality of your work?

1. ___   2. ___   3. ___   4. ___   5. ___   6. ___   7. ___   8. ___   9. ___   10. ___

THANKS FOR COMING ALONG

In the hundreds of seminars I have conducted over the years, I typically include several "one-sentence zingers" sprinkled throughout. Often these gems provide more sage advice to the educators in the trenches than the six or seven hours I will have spent with them. It seems appropriate that I close this book in the same manner. Starting with my very favorite, and then in no particular order, I share the rest. All of these closely relate to our becoming data driven with the goal of providing a high-quality instructional program. If no name accompanies the quote, I'm afraid it's mine.

- *In times of change, learners inherit the earth while the learned are beautifully equipped to deal with a world that no longer exists.*—Eric Hoffer

    In this world of rapid change, a world in which tomorrow will be completely different from today, how can we argue that education should not be keeping up. Educators who are unwilling to continue their learning only have a job, not a profession. And change, as a profession, we must. This book carries a small dose to help you on your way.

- *If you can't own part of a problem, you'll never own any of the solution.*

    When we accept a problem as ours, we are much more likely to seriously engage in finding a solution than when we claim no part of the cause. This is so true when it comes to the achievement level of our students. When we point fingers as to why we didn't make our NCLB standard, claiming no responsibility, the likelihood of becoming enthusiastic about new plans is very small.

- *Those who exercise their right to criticize must accept their responsibility to create.*

    It takes little brain power to criticize and complain. We should pay far more attention to those who are willing to take the problem a step further and offer solutions following their criticism.

- *Every student we send to Harvard or Stanford is offset by every student we let fall through the cracks.*

    It is right to take some of the credit when our students succeed, only when we also claim partial responsibility for our students' failures. How many of us believe that our 15 students who enter an acclaimed university are quickly offset by the 15 who dropped out of our high school?

- Insanity: *Endlessly repeating the same process, hoping for different results.* —Albert Einstein

    Offering a fresh approach to data utility was the purpose of this book.

- *Action in absence of belief is a wasted asset!*—Author unknown

    Passion prevails when we do something we strongly believe in. Going through the motions with little enthusiasm benefits very few.

- *Never doubt that a small group of thoughtful, committed citizens can change the world. Indeed, it is the only thing that ever has.*—Margaret Mead

  Substitute "educators" in the place of "citizens." Does it work for you? Perhaps then we could claim the second part of Mead's statement.

- *We need to keep inventing wheels, not because we need more wheels, but because we need more inventors.*—Bruce Joyce

  "Continuous improvement" and "producing high quality" were operative phrases throughout this book. Our passion as professionals will be reflected by our individual and corporate thirst to be better. The Mead and Einstein quotes remind us to be inventors.

Resource A

Reproducible Tools

The figure below shows where along the quality continuum each of the tools fits. The "Three Faces of Quality," the right portion of the figure are supported by Tools 1–4. Planning is supported by an additional four, Tools 6–9, and Capacity Building's Tool 10 completes the picture. Tool 5, Collaboration, is a part of the entire process.

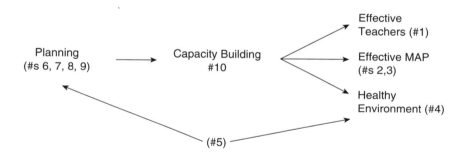

Tool 1: Analysis of My Teaching Characteristics

Tool 2: Analysis of Our MAP—The Support/Deterrent Approach

Tool 3: Analysis of Our MAP—The Rubric Approach

Tool 4: The Nine-Factor Profile

Tool 5: A Collaboration Rubric

Tool 6: Checklist for Effective Planning

Tool 7: Essential Agreements

Tool 8: The Implementation Guide

Tool 9: The Quality and Doability of the Plan

Tool 10: Capacity-Building Evaluation Form

TOOL 1: ANALYSIS OF MY TEACHING CHARACTERISTICS

Several elements of one's teaching can support or detract from the overall quality of the teaching process. Identifying these supports and deterrents will assist a teacher in deciding which areas to address in order to continuously improve.

Directions: Identify the instructional program in which the assessment is being made. Seventeen characteristics of effective teaching are listed down the left side of the table below. The "Description" column clarifies the characteristic. In the "Rating" column, record one of two symbols for each characteristic. The "Comments" column provides space to record anything the teacher wants to highlight. *Be sure to address the program in question.*

A "+" indicates that the element currently supports the quality of my teaching.
A "−" indicates that the element currently is a deterrent to the quality of my teaching.
A "?" indicates uncertainty.

Instructional Program _____

Characteristic	Description	Rating + or − or ?	Comments
Maintains high expectations for *all* students	Behavior reflects the value that "All of my students will achieve. I expect it!" Distinguishes between high expectations and unreasonable standards. Expectations go well beyond grading. Does not have an unrealistic grading standard. This means *all* students.	1	
Clear, focused, well-planned instructional lessons	Teacher is well organized; planning focuses on the lesson to be learned; teacher makes certain that instructional materials are aligned with intended learning.	2	
Teacher is skilled in a variety of instructional strategies and has a solid knowledge of pedagogy	Instruction is varied; not "sameolesameole" each day. Teacher understands how students learn and creates lessons to align with this understanding. Teaching is an art as well as a science, and this is reflected in what this teacher does.	3	
Manages the classroom well; has discipline well in control	Consistency, fairness, clarity, communication to students are all part of this characteristic.	4	
Creates a positive classroom environment; the classroom is a pleasant place in which to be	Students look forward to coming to class; the class gets a "smiley face," without having a circus atmosphere. Students know they're here to learn, and the classroom environment invites learning.	5	
Teacher displays a caring, sensitive attitude toward the students	Teacher has a positive view of the students; teacher is possibly one to whom students would turn if they were experiencing a personal problem; avoids strong criticism of students, especially in a group setting	6	
Teacher has solid base of content knowledge in those areas being taught	The teacher understands the content; teacher's knowledge goes well beyond what is being taught.	7	
Teacher is positive and enthusiastic about his/her work; this transfers to the students	This goes beyond just being a nice, caring person. This relates to the content itself. "I am enthusiastic about what I am teaching. I bring life to the content," is what this characteristic is about.	8	
Teacher uses a different strategy to reteach a concept that the students didn't understand	When the teacher realizes that the students (or a student) have not understood, in his/her repertoire of strategies is a new way of looking at the issue. And if they don't get it again, perhaps there is a third way.	9	

TOOL 1: ANALYSIS OF MY TEACHING CHARACTERISTICS (CONTINUED)

Instructional Program _____

Characteristic	Description	Rating + or – or ?	Comments
Teacher understands the students and their characteristics; can put the content into context in order to make meaning for the students	Students have lives beyond school; they come from a variety of cultures and life styles. The teacher understands this. Lessons are geared to these differences, and practicality is a goal. Teaching is given a context.	10	
Teacher has a healthy sense of humor and carries this humor into the classroom	This sense of humor is part of #5 above. Humor is appropriate and contextual, often within the framework of the lesson.	11	
Teacher has a system of incentives and rewards for students	Rewards can be intrinsic or extrinsic. Rewards are purposeful and relate to the task at hand. Giving extra credit for bringing frogs to a biology class would not fit here. Nor would raising a grade for getting the most money for the jogathon do not fit here.	12	
Teacher has a grading system that reflects the goals of the course; system is fair in all respects	The teacher's grading system is communicated up front and continuously. Students always know why they got the grade they got on any assignment or at the end of any grading period. The grading system is never cast in stone.	13	
Teacher has system for monitoring student progress; uses the system as part of ongoing planning	Teacher rarely has to wonder whether the students understand a concept; continuous monitoring and checking for understanding is a part of the process . . . always!!	14	
Teacher uses a variety of assessment techniques; understands the importance of good assessment	Does not depend on one or two types of assessments like homework and tests. Assessment is planned, never a last-minute rush job. Teacher understands the difference between good and poor assessments	15	
Teacher self-evaluates and adjusts practices regularly; consistently trying to improve is one of the teacher's goals	Self-reflection is ongoing as the teacher assesses the quality of his/her work. Reflection can be micro (as in one lesson) or macro. Teacher owns failures; "blame" is not a part of the teacher's vocabulary.	16	
Teacher is very efficient in the use of classroom time. Students are consistently on task	Classroom runs like a well-oiled machine. Students create their own learning environments in which all are not necessarily doing the same thing, but all are in a learning mode. Minimum time is spent on things like checking attendance.	17	

(Continued)

TOOL 1: ANALYSIS OF MY TEACHING CHARACTERISTICS (CONTINUED)

SETTING PRIORITIES

Directions: Record a, +, or −, next to the 17 characteristics according to the teacher's assessment. Obtain these from the ratings above. Then identify the top three +'s and record them in the appropriate column below. Finally, rank the top three deterrents and place them in the blanks. A rank of "1" under the deterrent column represents the strongest deterrent; a "2" would be next; and so on.

1. _____ High expectations for *all* students

2. _____ Clear, focused, well-planned lessons

3. _____ Skilled in a variety of pedagogical instructional strategies; strong knowledge of pedagogy

4. _____ Manages classroom well; discipline well controlled.

5. _____ Positive classroom environment, a pleasant place to be

6. _____ A caring, sensitive attitude toward students

7. _____ Solid base of content knowledge

8. _____ Positive and enthusiastic about work

9. _____ Uses different strategies to reteach a concept that the students didn't understand

10. _____ Understands the students and their characteristics; puts lessons into context

11. _____ Has a healthy sense of humor

12. _____ Has a system of incentives and rewards

13. _____ Has a grading system reflecting the goals of the course; fair in all respects

14. _____ Has a system for monitoring student progress

15. _____ Uses a variety of assessment techniques; understands the importance of good assessment

16. _____ Self evaluates and adjusts practices regularly; consistently trying to improve

17. _____ Efficient in use of classroom time; students are consistently on task

Top Three Supports	Rank	Top Three Deterrents
	1st	
	2nd	
	3rd	

TOOL 2: ANALYSIS OF OUR MAP—THE SUPPORT/DETERRENT APPROACH

Several elements of a school program can support or detract from the quality of the program. Completing this Analysis of Our MAP (Materials-Actions-People) as a collaborative exercise identifies these elements. Completing "Setting Priorities" as closure to the exercise identifies the elements that need attention.

Directions: Fifteen elements of a program are listed down the left side of the table below. Space to add two more is available on the second page. The "Description" column clarifies the component. In the "Rating" column, record one of three symbols for each program component. The "Comments" column provides space to record anything the group wants to highlight.

(1) + indicates that the component currently supports the quality of the program.

(2) − indicates that the component currently is a deterrent to the quality of the program.

(3) 0 indicates that the component is not appropriate or relevant to assess.

Program being assessed _____

+ = Support
− = Deterrent
0 = Not assessed

Program Elements	Description	Rating	Comments
Materials/equipment for teachers (consider quality, quantity, accessibility)	Consider those things *specifically* for teacher use; e.g., teacher text editions, curriculum guides, professional books, journals, technology equipment	1	
Materials/equipment for students (consider quality, quantity, accessibility)	These, are items for student use; e.g., textbooks, supplemental books, technology, learning center equipment	2	
Materials/equipment for parents (consider quality, quantity, accessibility)	These are items specifically for parent use; e.g., kits for assisting students, materials for educating parents as to how to help students. Do not consider typical memos, newsletters, etc.	3	
Existing program content	Normally, this is in the form of curriculum standards; can be listed as instructional goals and objectives; also the content of the textbooks used	4	
Time spent on instruction (actual time spent teaching)	Consider only the time the teachers spend in direct contact with students. Is it understood and consistent across all teachers?	5	
Teachers' schedules (consider time for instruction, planning, duties, etc.)	Is there sufficient planning time? Reasonable duty time? Appropriate instructional time? Time to work together?	6	
Diagnosing learning and prescribing instruction on a student or group basis	Relates to the process of identifying where students are and adjusting instruction to meet individual and group needs. May be formal or informal. Does a process exist? Is it positive? Does the process assist or burden the teachers?	7	

(Continued)

TOOL 2: ANALYSIS OF OUR MAP—THE SUPPORT/DETERRENT APPRAOCH (CONTINUED)

Program being assessed _____

Program Elements	Description	Rating	Comments
Assessing student results or outcomes	Is there a system for assessing student progress? Is it efficient and effective? Consistent? Is assessment clearly connected to intended learnings? Efforts at performance-based assessment? Use of multiple measures? Do all teachers use and support the system?	8	
Organizing and operating the classroom	Is the manner in which classrooms are maintained efficient and effective? Is the organization basically sound in light of the number of students? Do teachers discuss issues related to classroom management?	9	
Physical facilities (library, classrooms, labs, etc.)	Do the facilities support effective instruction? (This would be significant for science, P.E., and other areas in which the physical plant facilities play an important role)	10	
Teachers' collective knowledge and skills in the area being assessed	While some teachers will be stronger than others, when we look across all teachers, are the knowledge and skills, collectively, a support or deterrent?	11	
Teachers' receptivity to the program	Do teachers agree with the intent of the program? Do they like the program? Is there an advocacy base for the program among the teachers?	12	
Collaboration among teachers	Do teachers meet regularly to discuss curriculum and instructional issues in the content area being assessed? Are skill building and coaching on the agendas?	13	
Staff development	Is there a strong link between staff development and what is planned for program implementation? Are staff development actions well received? Is there follow-through after formal workshop sessions?	14	
Communication systems (clear goals and expectations; understanding between principal, teachers, parents; articulation among the grades)	Do all levels within the school and community (especially the school) understand what is expected? Are lines of communication clear? Is it known who makes decisions and under what circumstances? Are there surprises? Is the situation fairly stable? What does curricular articulation among the grades look like?	15	
		16	
		17	

TOOL 2: ANALYSIS OF OUR MAP—THE SUPPORT/DETERRENT APPRAOCH (CONTINUED)

SETTING PRIORITIES

Program_____

Directions: Record a +, −, or 0 next to the 15 program elements according to the group's assessment. Obtain these from the ratings above. Then identify the top three +'s and record them in the appropriate column below. Finally, rank the top three deterrents and place them in the blanks. A rank of "1" under the "Deterrent" column represents the strongest deterrent; a "2" would be next; and so on.

_____ 1. Materials/equipment for teachers

_____ 2. Materials/equipment for students

_____ 3. Materials/equipment for parents

_____ 4. Existing program content

_____ 5. Time spent on instruction

_____ 6. Teachers' schedules

_____ 7. Diagnosing learning & prescribing instruction

_____ 8. Assessing student results

_____ 9. Organizing/operating the classroom

_____ 10. Physical facilities

_____ 11. Teachers' knowledge/skills

_____ 12. Teachers' receptivity

_____ 13. Collaboration

_____ 14. Staff development

_____ 15. Communication

TOP THREE SUPPORTS	RANK	TOP THREE DETERRENTS
	1ST	
_____	2ND	_____
_____	3RD	_____
_____		_____

TOOL 3: ANALYSIS OF OUR MAP—THE RUBRIC APPROACH

Instructional Program_____

Several elements of a school program can support or detract from the quality of the program. Completing this Analysis of Our MAP (Materials-Actions-People) as a collaborative exercise identifies these elements. Completing "Setting Priorities" as closure to the exercise identifies the elements that need attention.

Directions: Fifteen elements of a program are listed down the left side of the table below. The "Description" column clarifies the component. For each component, the group will select which of four descriptions best fits that particular component. Place the number of the description in the "Rating" box. Leave blank those that are not a part of the program (e.g., for some programs, the "materials and equipment for parents").

4 = This element is exceptionally strong. It could be described as in a category that is "above and beyond" what would normally be expected. Words that might come to mind when describing this component might be "exceptional," "excellent," or "exemplary."	3 = This element contributes to the overall quality of the program. While not among the strongest, it is seen as a positive factor. Improving this component would contribute to overall program improvement, but it is probably not a high-priority item. Words describing a component with this rating might be, "effective," "credible," or "meets expectations."	2 = This element has a history of mixed contribution to the overall quality of the program. While generally satisfactory, some parts can be strong while other parts are problematic. This one is really a mixed bag. Descriptive words might be, "developing," "questionable," or "uncertain."	1 = This element is in trouble; its contribution is definitely in the negative category. Words or phrases accompanying this rating would be "disappointing," "inadequate," "well below what we would hope for." There is little question among staff that this component is in need of improvement.

Program Elements	Description	Rating
1. Materials/equipment for teachers (consider quality, quantity, accessibility)	Consider those things *specifically* for teacher use; e.g., teacher text editions, curriculum guides, professional books, journals, technology equipment	
2. Materials/equipment for students (consider quality, quantity, accessibility)	These are items for student use; e.g., textbooks, supplemental books, technology, learning center equipment	
3. Materials/equipment for parents (consider quality, quantity, accessibility)	These are items specifically for parent use; e.g., kits for assisting students; materials for educating parents as to how to help students; do not consider typical memos, newsletters, etc.	
4. Existing program content	Normally, this is in the form of curriculum standards; can be listed as instructional goals and objectives; also the content of the textbooks used	
5. Time spent on instruction (actual time spent teaching)	Consider only the time the teachers spend in direct contact with students. Is it understood and consistent across all teachers?	
6. Teachers' schedules (consider time for instruction, planning, duties, etc.)	Is there sufficient planning time? Reasonable duty time? Appropriate instructional time? Time to work together?	

TOOL 3: ANALYSIS OF OUR MAP—THE RUBRIC APPROACH (CONTINUED)

Program Elements	Description	Rating
7. Diagnosing learning and prescribing instruction on a student or group basis	Relates to the process of identifying where students are and adjusting instruction to meet individual and group needs. May be formal or informal. Does a process exist? Is it positive? Does the process assist or burden the teachers?	
8. Assessing student results or outcomes	Is there a system for assessing student progress? Is it efficient and effective? Consistent? Is assessment clearly connected to intended learnings? Efforts at performance-based assessment? Use of multiple measures? Do all teachers use and support the system?	
9. Organizing and operating the classroom	Is the manner in which classrooms are maintained efficient and effective? Is the organization basically sound in light of the number of students? Do teachers discuss issues related to classroom management?	
10. Physical facilities (library, classrooms, labs, etc.)	Do the facilities support effective instruction? (This would be significant for science, P.E., and other areas in which the physical plant facilities play an important role.)	
11. Teachers' collective knowledge and skills in the area being assessed	While some teachers will be stronger than others, when we look across all teachers, are the knowledge and skills, collectively, a support or deterrent?	
12. Teachers' receptivity to the program	Do teachers agree with the intent of the program? Do they like the program? Is there an advocacy base for the program among the teachers?	
13. Collaboration among teachers	Do teachers meet regularly to discuss curriculum and instructional issues in the content area being assessed? Are skill building and coaching on the agendas?	
14. Staff development	Is there a strong link between staff development and what is planned for program implementation? Are staff development actions well received? Is there follow-through after formal workshop sessions?	
15. Communication systems (clear goals and expectations, understanding between principal, teachers, parents; articulation among the grades)	Do all levels within the school and community (especially the school) understand what is expected? Are lines of communication clear? Is it known who makes decisions and under what circumstances? Are there surprises? Is the situation fairly stable? What does curricular articulation among the grades look like?	

(Continued)

TOOL 3: ANALYSIS OF OUR MAP—
THE RUBRIC APPROACH (CONTINUED)

SETTING PRIORITIES

Based upon your ratings, *and the importance you attach to each of the elements* (some elements will be more important than others), list the four elements whose improvement you believe would affect most the overall quality of the instructional program.

1.   2.

3.   4.

If you were to pick just one for focusing your improvement, which would it be?

_____

TOOL 4: THE NINE-FACTOR PROFILE

	1	2	3	4	5	6	7	8	9
VERY HIGH									
MOD. HIGH									
SO-SO									
MOD. LOW									
VERY LOW									

1	2	3	4	5	6	7	8	9
Leader Support	Peer Advocacy	Defined Program	Monitor Implem.	Philoso-phical Agreement	Standards Expectations	Integration	Payoff Imple-menters	Feasibility

Necessary action to elevate the "health" of the profile:

(Continued)

TOOL 4: THE NINE-FACTOR PROFILE (CONTINUED)

Reading Your Profile—A Handy Helper

1. If leadership support (1) is 1½ or more ratings higher than peer advocacy (2), it appears to teachers to be mandated. This is not a good start.

2. If leadership support (1) and peer advocacy (2) are "so-so" or below, bets are that very little is happening.

3. If leadership support (1) is up and defined program (3), monitoring implementation (4), or standards and expectations (6), are "so-so" or below, confusion and irritation will surface among the teaching ranks, since they hear things but are confused about what they are hearing.

4. If leadership support (1) is up and philosophical agreement (5) is at least 1½ ratings lower, it's definitely seen as a mandate. Resistance is high.

5. If defined program (3) and standards and expectations (6) are so-so or below, there's probably not much communication going on, and if it is, it's the kind that's unproductive. There's undoubtedly quite a bit of confusion. You're likely to lose the program.

6. If defined program (3) and/or standards and expectations (6) are so-so or below and monitoring implementation (4) is relatively high, teachers are confused and angry. They believe they're being checked on or evaluated on something that's not clear. This is very unhealthy.

7. If monitoring implementation (4) is so-so or below, it is highly likely that very little is going on, regardless of what the rest of the profile looks like.

8. If payoff (8) is down, with an otherwise fairly healthy profile, it may appear that all is well, but initial enthusiasm will die off, especially if feasibility (9) is down.

9. If integration (7) and/or feasibility (9) are down, especially when leadership support (1) is high, teachers are saying, "It's too much!" Resistance will continue to grow and you'll lose it.

Suggested Steps for Reading a Profile

As you become more familiar (and confident) with using the profile, you will continue to discover new combinations that point to the future success/failure of a program. I have used the profile for several years, and I continue to discover new combinations that inform me. The steps through which I typically proceed to read a profile are listed below. They are *not* meant as absolutes, but they do provide a good start.

1. The relationship of #1, leadership support, to #2, teacher advocacy, is a first clue to what is happening with the program. If leadership support is 1½ or more ratings higher than teacher advocacy, the

TOOL 4: THE NINE-FACTOR PROFILE (CONTINUED)

*potentia*l for frustration and anger is there because the leader is more prominent than the teacher-leaders are. Remember, a leader can initiate a change, but a leader can never sustain it. Teacher advocacy becomes necessary.

2. Next, look at #5, philosophical agreement. If that rating is so-so or below, there's a good chance that things are not going well. But then, look at #2, teacher advocacy. If that is high, interventions may come more easily. Also look at the two clarity factors, 3 and 6. If they are not high, then the disagreement noted in #5 may be tentative. If we elevate #3 and #6, #5 could go up as well.

3. Now combine the results of Steps 1 and 2 above, and your prediction becomes clearer. If leadership support is high, teacher advocacy is lower, and there is a philosophical issue—we begin to see anger and frustration setting in. If these three are relatively high, we're off to a good start.

4. From there, look at #4, monitoring implementation. If #4 is high (relatively speaking), we want to know if that high 4 is supportive or threatening. It is threatening if teachers believe they had no role (high 1, lower 2), if there is no teacher voice (low 2), and/or there is philosophical opposition (low 5); if any of those conditions exist, rebellion is close at hand. Teacher talk says, "We are being continuously checked on something that we had no part in designing and/or we don't yet believe in. You've got to be kidding. Take a hike!!"

5. If #4 is relative low, all the other ratings don't really matter, because, rather than anger, the dominant feeling will likely be ambivalence, accompanied by a "been there, done that" attitude. If #4 is high and 1, 2, and 5 are favorable, the outlook is good. Adjustments may be needed, but the atmosphere will be positive.

6. Look at #3, clarity of program, and #6, standards and expectations for implementation. If these are so-so or below, confusion is the result. Confusion is okay if leadership support, teacher advocacy, and philosophical agreement are generally present, because the confusion can be cleared up. But if these are so-so and below and monitoring implementation is high, we've got trouble.

7. If after the above six, we see we're in trouble, the latter factors, 7, 8, and 9, become inconsequential. If after the six listed above, we're in pretty good shape, look at 8 and 9, payoff for teachers and program feasibility. The relative health of the program, as depicted by the profile, may not hold very long if the program is too complex and a lot of work for the teachers, even though initially it looks good. The fatigue factor enters in with too much work over an extended period of time.

TOOL 5: COLLABORATION RUBRIC (CONTINUED)

	Desired	**Starting Out**
Established philosophy	We believe that ours is no longer a closed-door profession. We view collaboration as an essential resource for solving problems and elevating the quality of our work. We know we are better together than we are individually. Disagreement is healthy. We hold ourselves accountable for the learning of *all* students, not just those in our classroom. We believe that "celebration" should not be an uncommon word among us. We celebrate being a "staff of one."	Collaboration is not thought about as something requiring philosophical consideration. We work positively together on things like school plans, but will typically yield to lead teachers or to our principal when difficulty or disagreements occur. We're pretty much concerned about the achievement of our own kids in our classrooms, and see talking to others about their kids at best as "something interesting, but not about me."
Leadership/ role of principal	Our principal "walks the talk" regarding collaboration. Time is allocated for working together and is held "sacred." Leaders model collaborative strategies as the group consciously focuses on shared goals. District and school leaders are responsive to stated needs. Training and assistance are ongoing.	Our principal is helpful in arranging to get teachers together when something is to be accomplished, but his/her behavior does not communicate the essential nature of collaboration. There is no "marketing" or promotion of the advantages of the practice as "the way we do business."
Ownership	We are interdependent; collectively and independently we hold ourselves accountable for the quality of our work and for student results. It is "our success" or "our failure." We foster a culture of mutual trust and respect. All contributions are valued, as using the language of respect is a norm. Closed-door autonomy is a thing of the past.	We focus pretty much on our own classroom. Our profession in action is "my kids and I, in the classroom, all doing the best we can." When assuming responsibility for our work, we typically speak as an "I," not as a "we." Blaming or citing things beyond our control as reasons for some of our challenges is not necessarily the rule, but it is not uncommon.
Nature of sharing	Sharing focuses on common goals and mutual responsibility. When we come together, we talk about student learning, benchmark assessments, evidence of student learning, "at risk" students, successful and unsuccessful strategies. The word "blame" is not in our vocabulary . . . we have no pity parties.	Sharing almost seems a contrived activity. We do it, but to what end? To do something better or to get a job done? We do not resist it; we rather enjoy it. But it really isn't an integral part of our work on a continuous basis.
Clarity of expectations	Time for collaboration is carefully structured. All teachers understand their role and responsibilities. There is no confusion about outcomes or "Why are we here?" We know that we are about shared planning, problem solving, new strategies, and interventions for at-risk students, in an ongoing way. This is the way we do business, even when no one's watching.	The description to the left in the "Desired" column is not uncommon for a single activity, such as when we write our school plan. But when left to our own natural m/o, we would not operate this way. The difference between "Desired" and "Starting Out" is that here, it is not the way we do business; it is not continuous when no one's watching.
Strategies	Our collaborative strategies are varied; we understand that there are several ways that collaboration can occur on a campus; we go well beyond "meeting and conferring." We may try teaming, coteaching, peer coaching, lesson study; in addition to collaborating about important student issues, we "collaborate about collaboration." We work to get better at it.	We don't consider collaboration has having strategies. Collaboration is coming together to discuss issues, perhaps to reach decisions of one kind or another, and then going our way. We would not view the examples included in the "Desired" column to the left as collaboration, and we would never think of behaving in this manner on our own.

TOOL 5: COLLABORATION RUBRIC (CONTINUED)

Directions: Carefully read the descriptions provided under "Starting Out" and "Desired" for each component. Create the profile that you believe best describes the degree of collaborative practices at your site by placing a point on each of the six lines representing the six collaborative categories. By visually connecting the points, you will have established a "collaboration profile" from which to plan accordingly.

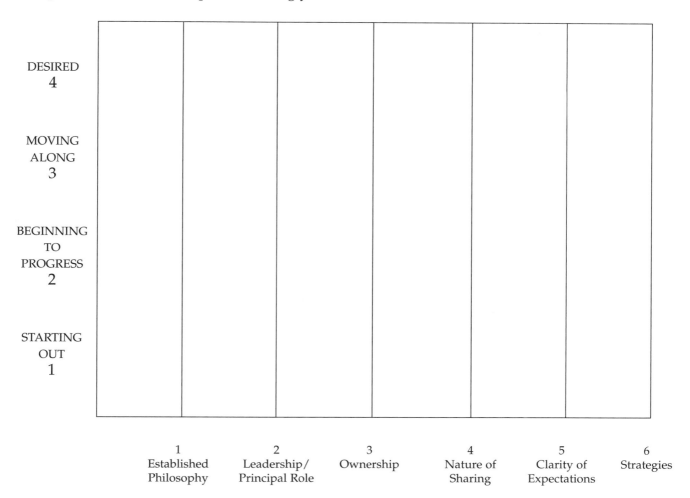

1	2	3	4	5	6
Established Philosophy	Leadership/ Principal Role	Ownership	Nature of Sharing	Clarity of Expectations	Strategies

Overall assessment of our collaborative process and recommendations for next steps to continuously improve our process:

TOOL 6: CHECKLIST FOR EFFECTIVE PLANNING

Characteristics of the Checklist for Effective Planning

It is important for planning activities to be positive. Effective planning will yield a favorable prognosis for success of a program while questionable planning practices will create difficulty quickly.

When a group is aware of the contributors to effective planning and monitors the presence of these contributors, formally or informally, a step closer to high-quality program accountability will have been taken.

Below is a list of 14 contributors to effective planning. Considering *your personal preferences* and the *conditions of your work site*, select those that are the most important for you. Place a check in the blanks of those you consider the most important. Be very selective with your checks. No more than 5 or 6 would be preferable.

Planning Checklist

Organization of the Planning Process

1. ____ "Planning to plan" session: Refers to a meeting to discuss how planning will occur; objectives, group processes, decision making, conflict resolution, expected outcomes, and the like would be determined.

2. ____ Written norms: The group has a set of established ground rules regarding how the group will operate when they are together.

3. ____ Group facilitator: Person is identified to lead the process and responsibilities are established.

4. ____ Objectives for planning: The group knows what the purpose of each planning session is, what the expected outcomes are, and is aware of its roles and responsibilities.

5. ____ Conflict resolution: Procedures for resolving differences of opinion are established ahead of time.

6. ____ Decision making: Procedures are in place to enable fair and consistent decision making. How decisions are made is determined ahead of time, e.g., majority rule or consensus.

7. ____ Group members' roles and responsibilities: These are clear and understood by all group members; the degree of decision-making authority (empowerment) is known; constraints are understood.

TOOL 6: CHECKLIST FOR EFFECTIVE PLANNING (CONTINUED)

8. ____ Materials available for reference: During the planning session, materials, including current data, are available for reference; this is to enhance the efficiency, hence the effectiveness, of the planning sessions.

9. ____ Contribution of research to the plan: Known research findings are considered when formulating the plan; when solutions are posed, the group questions itself regarding the basis upon which the strategies were formulated.

Group Interaction

10. ____ Group members' contribution: There is positive contribution from each group member, using the language of respect; the group holds itself responsible for obtaining input from everyone while a planning meeting is in progress.

11. ____ Continual refocusing: During planning sessions, it is an understood responsibility of everyone to refocus when the group is getting off target (or "bird walking").

12. ____ Member domination: There will no domination by any group member or members; the group sees this as an essential characteristic of an effective process.

Supportive Elements

13. ____ Time: There is sufficient time to plan, both on a short-term (one session) and a long-term (entire process) basis.

14. ____ Availability of resources: Such aspects as released time, selected personnel, and the access to materials are considered and made available according to the significance of the task.

Thank you for sharing your thoughts. Record your preferences on the form that has been provided. From the data on this form, we will select those characteristics that will become our standards for planning.

TOOL 6: CHECKLIST FOR EFFECTIVE PLANNING (CONTINUED)

Arriving at the list: To arrive at the desirable set of planning contributors, proceed as follows. The whole activity takes about 30 minutes.

1. Each member of the planning team completes the Planning Checklist (see further below).

2. Record the preferences on the tabulation sheet below.

3. Each member then shares his/her selections indicating why these choices were made and not others.

4. Record the group consensus in the column on the right. *This becomes the final list!*

Characteristics	Rater 1	Rater 2	Rater 3	Rater 4	Rater 5	Rater 6	Rater 7	Rater 8	Consensus (Check those that will be used)
1									
2									
3									
4									
5									
6									
7									
8									
9									
10									
11									
12									
13									
14									

TOOL 7: ESSENTIAL AGREEMENTS

Areas of Implementation	Essential Agreements:_____ Program:_____

Checklist for Mentoring

Areas of Implementation	Teacher 1	Teacher 2	Teacher 3	Teacher 4	Teacher 5	Teacher 6	Teacher 7	Teacher 8	Teacher 9	Teacher 10

Identified needs for implementation improvement and plans to do so:

_____

_____

_____

_____

TOOL 8: THE IMPLEMENTATION GUIDE

Components	Ideal		Transitory		Just for Starters	
	3		2		1	
	3		2		1	
	3		2		1	
	3		2		1	

(Continued)

TOOL 8: THE IMPLEMENTATION GUIDE (CONTINUED)

This form is to collect teacher self-reports from use of the Implementation Guide, whose skeletal structure is shown above. The result of using this form will be similar to that shown in Chapter 3. Place a 3, 2, or 1 in each cell for each teacher.

Information provided by this aggregation of teacher-supplied information is to be used to further the implementation effort.

	Components (use one-word abbreviations to label the columns)					
	1._____	2._____	3._____	4._____	5._____	6._____
Teacher 1						
Teacher 2						
Teacher 3						
Teacher 4						
Teacher 5						
Teacher 6						
Teacher 7						
Teacher 8						
Teacher 9						
Teacher 10						
Teacher 11						
Teacher 12						
Teacher 13						
Teacher 14						
Teacher 15						
Teacher 16						
Teacher 17						
Teacher 18						
Teacher 19						
Teacher 20						

TOOL 9: THE QUALITY AND DOABILITY OF THE PLAN

Directions: For each of the questions, assess the degree to which the proposed program is better than the program currently being implemented. Place a check in the column of choice. When completed, answer the two questions at the bottom.

Sometimes a proposed plan is an extension of what currently exists. If that is the case, assess how much the proposed plan adds to program quality.

If for some reason a question is not relevant to ask, mark this in the last column.

Questions for Consideration	New Plan Much Better	New Plan Somewhat Better	No Real Difference	Current Program Somewhat Better	Current Program Much Better	Not a Relevant Question
1. When comparing the materials and equipment for teachers, which fares better?						
2. When comparing the materials and equipment for students, which fares better?						
3. When considering curriculum content and the relationship to our standards, which fares better?						
4. When considering the time that will be spent on instruction (the actual time teaching), which fares better?						
5. Considering the whole area of assessment (diagnosing deficiencies, assessing and monitoring student progress, final assessment), which program fares better?						
6. Which program fares better relative to planned staff development?						
7. Which program do the teachers prefer?						
8. Which of the two programs is the easiest to implement?						
9. Which of the two programs fosters opportunities for teacher collaboration?						
10. What is the assessment by the school principal of the quality of the two programs?						
11. Which of the two programs do the teacher leaders in the school prefer?						
12. Which of the two programs is easier to monitor and support the implementation of the program?						
13. Which of the two programs is clearer and more understandable to teachers?						
14. Which of the two programs will likely produce the higher level of student achievement?						
15.						
16.						

FROM OUR ANSWERS TO THE QUESTIONS, (1) IS IT PROBABLE THAT THE PROPOSED PLAN WILL PRODUCE A HIGHER-QUALITY PROGRAM THAN THAT CURRENTLY IN EXISTENCE? AND (2) KNOWING THE CONDITIONS OF OUR WORK SITE, IS THE PROPOSED PLAN FEASIBLE

1. ___ YES!!   ___ Yes   ___ Uncertain   ___ No   ___ NO!!
2. ___ YES!!   ___ Yes   ___ Uncertain   ___ No   ___ NO!!

TOOL 10: CAPACITY-BUILDING EVALUATION FORM

Topic of Session_____

Date_____ Your Staff Category_____

The purpose of capacity-building sessions is to present information and strategies that will assist in change or new implementation. Input concerning these sessions is extremely important to future planning.

You will be provided with a list of outcomes/objectives that corresponds to the numbers listed on the left of the Rating Table. Please rate each on a scale from 4 to 1 according to the descriptors provided.

In each of the three categories on the Rating Table, place a check that best indicates your opinions.

There will be three checks for each outcome/objective.

Outcomes/ Objectives	Degree of Understanding				Value to Me				Readiness for Implementation			
	High Degree 4	3	2	Low Degree 1	Very Valuable 4	3	2	Little Value 1	Ready 4	3	2	Not Ready 1
1												
2												
3												
4												
5												
6												
7												
8												

Comment:

Resource B

Sources of Characteristics of Effective Teachers

Title	Author/Source	Identified Characteristics of Effective Teachers
"A Study of Fifty Effective Teachers Whose Average Gain Scores Ranked in the Top 15% of Each of Four School Types in Project STAR"	Bain, H. P., Lintz, N., & Word, E. (1989, April). Paper presented at the annual meeting of the American Education Research Association (AERA), San Francisco.	1. Uses a variety of instructional planning activities, teaching strategies, and materials 2. Has high expectations of students 3. Uses clear, focused instruction 4. Monitors student progress 5. Reteaches with alternate strategies 6. Uses incentives and rewards 7. Has highly efficient classroom routines 8. Has high standards of classroom behavior 9. Has excellent personal interactions with students
Developing Effective Teaching Skills (p. 40)	Butcher, J. (2004). [electronic version] New York: Routledge Falmer. Retrieved from Questia.com	1. Establishes and maintains an effective learning environment where students feel secure and confident, and where diversity is valued 2. Organizes and manages teaching/learning time appropriately 3. Plans and structures learning activities 4. Communicates effectively with learners 5. Reviews the learning process with learners 6. Selects and develop resources to support learning 7. Has high expectations of all pupils 8. Treats students consistently, with respect and consideration 9. Recognizes and responds effectively to equal opportunities issues that arise in the classroom, including challenging stereotyped views, bullying, and harassment 10. Demonstrates and promotes positive values, attitudes, and behaviors that are expected from students
California Standards for the Teaching Profession	California Commission on Teacher Credentialing (1997). California Department of Education.	Engaging and Supporting *All* Students in Learning 1. Connects students' prior knowledge, life experience, and interests with learning goals 2. Uses a variety of instructional strategies and resources to respond to the students' diverse needs 3. Facilitates learning experiences that promote autonomy, interaction, and choice 4. Engages students in problem solving, critical thinking, and other activities that make subject matter meaningful 5. Promotes self-directed, reflective learning for *all* students

Creating and Maintaining Effective Environments for Student Learning
1. Creates a physical environment that engages all students
2. Promotes social development and group responsibility
3. Establishes and maintains standards for student behavior
4. Plans and implements classroom procedures and routines that support student learning
5. Uses instructional time effectively

Understanding and Organizing Subject Matter for Student Learning
1. Demonstrates knowledge of subject matter content and student development
2. Organizes curriculum to support student understanding of subject matter
3. Interrelates ideas and information within and across subject matter areas
4. Develops student understanding through instructional strategies that are appropriate to the subject matter
5. Uses materials, resources, and technologies to make subject matter accessible to students.

Planning Instruction and Designing Learning Experiences for *All* Students
1. Draws on and values students' backgrounds, interests, and developmental learning needs
2. Establishes and articulates goals for student learning
3. Develops and sequences instructional activities and materials for student learning
4. Designs short- and long-term plans to foster student learning
5. Modifies instructional plans to adjust for student needs

Assessing Student Learning
1. Establishes and communicates learning goals for *all* students
2. Collects and uses multiple sources of information to assess student learning
3. Involves and guides all students in assessing their own learning
4. Uses the results of assessment to guide instruction
5. Communicates with students, families, and other audiences about student progress

(Continued)

Title	Author/Source	Identified Characteristics of Effective Teachers
		Developing as a Professional Educator 1. Reflects on teaching practice and plans professional development 2. Establishes professional goals and pursues opportunities to grow professionally 3. Works with communities to improve professional practice 4. Works with families to improve professional practice 5. Works with colleagues to improve professional practice 6. Balances professional responsibilities and maintains motivation
"Elements of a Model of Effective Teachers" [Abstract]	Clark, J. C., & Walsh, J. (n.d.). Retrieved on April 4, 2005, from: http://www.aare.edu.au/02pap/wal02220.html	1. Content knowledge 2. Pedagogical skills 3. Strong relationships with students 4. Firm moral code 5. Knowledge of the context in which they were teaching 6. Curriculum knowledge 7. Pedagogical content knowledge 8. Knowledge of learners and their characteristics 9. Collaboration with colleagues and community 10. Sphere of influence beyond the classroom 11. A change agent 12. Oriented to improved student learning (Classified into [1] content knowledge, [2] pedagogical knowledge and skills; [3] knowledge and context; [4] personal knowledge.)
Effective Schooling Practices: A Research Synthesis 1995 Update	Cotton, K. (1995). [Electronic version] Portland, OR: Northwest Regional Education Laboratory. Retrieved from: http://www.nwrel.org/scpd/esp/esp95.html	1. Preplanned curriculum 2. Curriculum integration 3. Grouping to fit students' needs 4. Efficient use of time 5. Efficient routines 6. Behavior standards 7. Orientation to lessons 8. Clear and focused instruction 9. Feedback and reinforcement 10. Review and reteaching 11. Thinking-skills instruction 12. Efficient questioning techniques

Source	Reference	Characteristics
		13. Workplace-readiness skills integrated 14. High expectations for student learning 15. Incentives, recognition, and rewards 16. Positive personal interactions 17. Equity (high-needs students attended to; fosters resiliency; creates intergroup harmony) 18. Monitors student progress 19. Uses alternative assessments
Characteristics of Effective Teachers	Eble, K. (1970). Salt Lake City, UT: Project to Improve College Teaching.	1. Takes an analytic/synthetic approach 2. Organized and clear 3. Teacher/group interaction 4. Teacher/individual student interaction 5. Enthusiastic
"New Imperatives for Teacher Education"	Education Commission of the States. (2000, October–November). *The Progress of Education Reform.* Retrieved April 5, 2005, from http://www.ecs.org/clearing house/22/38/2238.html	1. Subject matter knowledge 2. Knowledge of educational theory 3. Pedagogical skills 4. Emphasizes hands-on learning, higher-order thinking skills, and individualized instruction
"Characteristics of Effective Teachers"	Hasenstab, J. J. (n.d.). *Heart of Teaching, 79.* Retrieved from http://www.plsweb.com/resources/newsletters/hot_arch ives/79/effective_teachers/	1. Expresses him- or herself positively 2. Communicates with interest and enthusiasm 3. Employs direct eye contact 4. Questions, directions, statements are clear 5. Is empathetic 6. Limits new information 7. Explains and illustrates concepts both abstractly and concretely 8. Teaches sequentially and globally 9. Asks thought-provoking questions 10. Employs a wide variety of methods 11. Has a sense of humor 12. Is sensitive

(Continued)

(Continued)

Title	Author/Source	Identified Characteristics of Effective Teachers
		13. Maintains poise when something goes wrong 14. Avoids aggravation 15. Uses rewards, intrinsic and extrinsic
"Effective Teachers of Numeracy in the Early Years and Beyond"	McDonough, A., & Clarke, D. (2003). Describing the practice of effective teachers of mathematics in the early years. In N. A. Pateman, B. J. Dougherty, & J. Zilliox (Eds.), *Proceedings of then International Group for the Psychology of Mathematics Education* (Vol. 3, pp. 261–268), Honolulu: University of Hawaii, College of Education.	1. Preplanned curriculum 2. High expectations for student learning 3. Students are carefully oriented to their lessons 4. Instruction is clear and focused 5. Learning progress is monitored 6. Reteaching occurs 7. Class time is used for learning 8. Smooth, efficient classroom routines 9. Use of instructional groups 10. Standards for behavior are explicit 11. Positive personal interaction between teacher and students 12. Incentives and rewards are used to promote excellence
Ten Traits of Highly Effective Teachers: How to Hire, Coach, and Mentor Effective Teachers	McEwan, E. (2002). Thousand Oaks, CA: Corwin Press.	The 10 traits fall into 3 distinct categories: personal traits (character), teaching traits (get results), intellectual traits (demonstrate knowledge, awareness, self-understanding) 1. Passionate; mission driven 2. Positive and real 3. Teacher-leader 4. "With-it-ness" 5. Style 6. Motivational expertise 7. Instructional effectiveness 8. Book-learning trait 9. Street smarts 10. A mental life
Research on Teacher Performance Criteria	Rosenshine., B., & Furst, M. (1971). In B. O. Smith (Ed.), *Research in teacher education* (pp. 37–72). Englewood Cliffs, NJ: Prentice Hall.	Rosenshine and Furst's meta-analysis in 1971 identified 10 characteristics: 1. Clarity (requires planning and organization) 2. Variability; adding variety to teaching techniques 3. Enthusiasm (students will only be as enthusiastic as you are) 4. Task-oriented, businesslike behavior (takes teaching seriously)

	5. Positive reinforcement (acknowledge students' ideas; actually uses them; verbal rewards; creates a "can-do attitude" 6. Student opportunity to learn (were the students given the information they needed?) 7. Avoids strong criticism (no put downs) 8. Structured comments (provides an overview of what happened or what is about to happen) 9. Effective questioning (use to enhance critical thinking; wait time; call on students w/o a pattern; probe) 10. Humor (acts as a motivator; demonstrates enjoyment of work; adds variety to class)	
"Possibilities and Challenges: The National Board for Professional Teaching Standards"	1. Committed to students and their learning 2. Subject matter knowledge and how to teach to those subjects 3. Manages and monitors student learning 4. Thinks systematically about his or her practices; learns from experiences 5. Member of learning communities	Retrieved from: http://www.aare.edu.au/02pap/wal02220.htm
"Nurturing Five Dispositions of Effective Teachers"	1. Empathy 2. Positive view of others 3. Positive view of self 4. Authenticity 5. Meaningful purpose and vision	Usher, B. S., Usher, M., & Usher, D. (2003, November). 2nd National Symposium on Educator Dispositions, Eastern Kentucky University, Richmond.
"Summary of Major Concepts Covered by Harry K. Wong"	1. Good classroom management skills 2. Teaches for mastery 3. Positive expectations for student success	Wong, H. (n.d.). Retrieved April 6, 2005, from http://www.glavac.com/harrywong.html

References

Alkin, M. C., & Christie, C. A. (2004). *Evaluation roots (Tracing theorists' views and influences)*. Thousand Oaks, CA: Sage.

Bernhardt, V. L. (2004, November–December). Continuous improvement: It takes more than test scores. *ACSA Leadership*, 16–19.

Bernhardt, V. L. (2005). *Using data to improve student learning in school districts*. Larchmont, NY: Eye on Education.

Bracey, G. W. (2000). *Bail me out! Handing difficult data and tough questions about public schools*. Thousand Oaks, CA: Corwin Press.

Chapman, D. W., & Carrier, C. A. (Eds.). (1990). *Improving educational quality: A global perspective*. Westport, CT: Greenwood Press.

Creighton, T. B. (2001). *Schools and data*. Thousand Oaks, CA: Corwin Press.

DuFour, R. (1998). *Professional learning communities at work*. Bloomington, IN: National Educational Service.

Educational Research Service. (2004). *The informed educator: Harnessing the power of teacher collaboration to increase student learning*. Arlington, VA: Educatioal Research Service.

Fullan, M. (1982). *The meaning of educational change*. New York: Teachers College Press.

Fullan, M. (1991). *The new meaning of educational change*. New York: Teachers College Press.

Fullan, M. (1993). *Change forces*. Bristol, PA: Falmer.

Fullan, M. (2003). *The moral imperative of leadership*. Thousand Oaks, CA: Corwin Press.

Hall, G., & Hord, S. (2006). *Implementing change: Patterns, principles, and potholes*. Boston: Pearson.

Harvey, T. R. (1990). *Checklist for change*. Needham Heights, MA: Allyn & Bacon.

Holcomb, E. L. (2001). *Asking the right questions* (2nd ed.). Thousand Oaks, CA: Corwin Press.

Holcomb, E. L. (2004). *Getting excited about data* (2nd ed.). Thousand Oaks, CA: Corwin Press.

Hord, S. M., Rutherford, W. L., Huling-Austin, L. L., & Hall, G. E. (1987). *Taking charge of change*. Alexandria, VA: Association for Supervision and Curriculum Development.

Huberman, A. M., & Miles, M. B. (1984). *Innovation up close: How school improvement works*. New York: Plenum.

Isaac, S., & Michael, W. B. (1995). *Handbook in research and evaluation . . . for education and the behavioral sciences* (3rd ed.). San Diego, CA: Educational and Industrial Testing Services.

Jason, M. H. (2003). *Evaluating programs to increase student achievement*. Thousand Oaks, CA: Corwin Press.

Johnson, R. S. (2002). *Using data to close the achievement gap*. Thousand Oaks, CA: Corwin Press.

Kaufman, R., Guerra, I., & Platt, W. A. (2006). *Practical evaluation for educators.* Thousand Oaks, CA: Corwin Press.

Leithwood, K., Aitken, R., & Jantzi, D. (2006). *Making schools smarter* (3rd ed.). Thousand Oaks, CA: Corwin Press.

Marzano, R. (2003). *What works in schools: Translating research into action.* Alexandria, VA: Association for Supervision and Curriculum Development.

McEwan, E. K. (2003). *7 steps to effective instructional leadership* (2nd ed.). Thousand Oaks, CA: Corwin Press.

National Commission on Excellence in Education. (1983). *A nation at risk: The imperative for educational reform.* Washington, DC: U.S. Government Printing Office.

Parsons, B. A. (2002). *Evaluative inquiry.* Thousand Oaks, CA: Corwin Press.

Popham, J. (February 2003). *Trouble with testing* [Electronic version]. American School Boards Journal, *199*, 2.

Provus, M. (1971). *Discrepancy evaluation.* Berkeley, CA: McCutchan Corporation.

Reeves, D. B. (2000). *Accountability in action* (2nd printing). Denver, CO: Advanced Learning Press.

Reeves, D. B. (2002). *The daily disciplines of leadership.* San Francisco: Jossey-Bass.

Reeves, D. B. (2006). *The learning leader.* Alexandria, VA: Association for Supervision and Curriculum Development.

Sanders, J. R., & Sullins, C. D. (2006). *Evaluating school programs* (3rd ed.). Thousand Oaks, CA: Corwin Press.

Sarason, S. B. (1990). *The predictable failure of educational reform.* San Francisco: Jossey-Bass.

Sashkin, M., & Kiser, K. J. (1991). *Total quality management.* Seabrook, MD: Ducochon Press.

Schmoker, M. (1996). *Results.* Alexandria, VA: Association for Supervision and Curriculum Development.

Scriven, M. (1991). *Evaluation thesaurus* (4th ed.). Thousand Oaks, CA: Sage.

Senge, P. (1999). *The dance of change.* New York: Doubleday.

Sergiovanni, T. J. (1996). *Leadership for the schoolhouse: How is it different? Why is it important?* San Francisco: Jossey-Bass.

Stufflebeam, D. (1983). The CIPP model for program evaluation. In G. F. Madaus, M. Scriven, & D. L. Stufflebeam (Eds.), *Educational models* (Chap. 7, pp. 117–141). Boston: Kluwer-Nijhoff.

Technical Design Group of the Advisory Committee for the Public Schools Accountability Act of 1999. (2005). *Descriptive statistics and correlations tables for California's 2004 School Characteristics Index and similar schools ranks* (p. 2). Available at: http://cde.ca.gov

Warwick, R. (1995). *Beyond piecemeal improvements.* Bloomington, IN: National Educational Service.

Wiggins, G., & McTighe, J. (1998). *Understanding by design.* Alexandria, VA: Association for Supervision and Curriculum Development.

Index

CORWIN
PRESS